Piggyback Songs–
School Days

Ages 3–6

Published by Totline® Publications
an imprint of
Frank Schaffer Publications®

Totline®
PUBLICATIONS
™

Editor: Kim Bradford
Interior Designer: Jannette M. Bole

Frank Schaffer Publications®

Totline Publications is an imprint of Frank Schaffer Publications.

Send all inquiries to:
Frank Schaffer Publications
3195 Wilson Drive NW
Grand Rapids, Michigan 49544

Piggyback Songs: School Days—Ages 3–6

ISBN: 1-57029-521-2

1 2 3 4 5 6 7 8 9 10 10 09 08 07 06 05

Table of Contents

Introduction

Sing a song with children, and several great things happen: You have a merry time together, your children learn, and you pass along a love for music.

This book is full of songs to help make seasons and holidays fun. The songs are written to the tunes of childhood favorites and marked with guitar chords, making them easy to sing. (Note: Songs set to the tunes of "Frere Jacques" and "Row, Row, Row Your Boat" only have one chord listed so that they may be played and sung in rounds.) All songs have been organized by season and holiday and are labeled on the bottom outside edge of each page for easy access.

There are several Spanish-language songs in this book. Each of these songs is accompanied by a clearly marked Spanish pronunciation guide and an English translation.

Another special feature is the inclusion of some illustrated sign language. The term "sign language" is a generic term that indicates any form of manual communication. There are many different sign language systems, but American Sign Language (ASL) is the native language of most deaf Americans. It is a visual, gestural language with its own grammatical rules and is not a direct word-for-word representation of English. The signs in this book are a combination of ASL and English signs. Some signs were adapted for simplicity, and root words are represented without plural, possessive, or verb tense, such as s, 's, or -ing.

Songs play a unique role in helping young children learn. Involvement in music develops listening skills, nurtures creativity, and builds memory power. The fun word play and repetition of sounds within songs increase children's vocabulary and inspires a love for language. Enjoying silly songs together also encourages a child's developing sense of humor.

Early childhood educator Karen DeVries says there is much evidence of the benefits of songs and poetry in optimizing cognitive development, emotional peace and growth, and academic enrichment. Research shows similar results of how songs and poetry improve the brain's function and

cultivate growth. From the first parent lullaby, clearly, the benefits of music in a child's development are tremendous.

Music "connects" children in many ways in the early-elementary classroom. The music makes connections to content, emotions, peers, the teacher, and more "parts" that influence the "whole" child. A child doesn't listen to a teacher's off-key, perhaps even crackling, voice. A child listens to the gifts of joy and security in music, and a child hears the song within her own heart.

According to the National Association for Music Education (MENC), prekindergarten music instruction is critical for children's musical development and should provide opportunities to explore music with songs, movement, and instruments. Group music time is also encouraged as an important time for sharing music and making music together. The MENC Prekindergarten Standards addressed by the songs in this book include the following:

- Singing, alone and with others, a varied repertoire of music

- Performing on instruments, alone and with others, a varied repertoire of music

- Improvising melodies, variations, and accompaniments

- Listening to, analyzing, and describing music

Music is also a great way to address other early childhood standards. To help with your curriculum planning, this book includes icons that represent many key early childhood standards. The key for these icons is on page 5. You will see these icons throughout the book, next to the title of each song that addresses that standard. This way, you can integrate music and curricular instruction in one fun activity!

Singing is fun to do any time, so why not start right now? Just open the book, choose a song, and enjoy making music!

Early Learning Standards Icon Key

Language Development

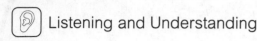

- 👂 Listening and Understanding
- 💬 Speaking and Communicating

Literacy

- Phonological Awareness
- Book Knowledge and Appreciation
- Print Awareness and Concepts
- Early Writing
- Alphabet Knowledge

Mathematics

- Number and Operations
- Geometry and Spatial Sense
- Patterns and Measurement

Science

- Scientific Knowledge

Approaches to Learning

- Initiative and Curiosity
- Reasoning and Problem Solving

Creative Arts

- Music
- Movement
- Dramatic Play

Social and Emotional Development

- Self-Concept
- Self-Control
- Cooperation
- Social Relationships
- Knowledge of Families and Communities

Physical Health and Development

- Gross-Motor Skills
- Fine-Motor Skills
- Health Status and Practices

1-57029-521-2 Piggyback Songs—School Days

Time for School

First Day of School

Sung to: I'm a Little Teapot

C   F   C
Good morning, Katie, how are you?

G7   C   G7   C
This is the very first day of school.

I'm so glad to meet you;

F   C
Others will be, too.

                F
Just come in the classroom,

        C   G7   C
There're lots of things to do.

Substitute the name of one of your children for the name Katie.

Kristina Carle and Nanette Belice
Kensington, MD

Brand New Year

Sung to: London Bridge

   C
It's time to start a brand new year,

G7   C
Brand new year, brand new year.

It's time to start a brand new year.

G7   C
Welcome, new friends.

C
We'll learn lots of brand new things,

G7   C
Brand new things, brand new
     things!

We'll learn lots of brand new things.

G7   C
Let's get started now.

Patricia Coyne
Mansfield, MA

Learn  Sign

At

With fingers together and palms out, bring right fingertips up to touch the back of the left hand.

Learn Sign

Our

Starting with cupped right hand on right side of chest, bring it around in an arc to the left so little finger touches right chest.

Working Together

Sung to: Here We Go Looby Loo

D
Let's all make a boat.

        A7
Let's all make a boat.

D
Let's all make a boat

A7   D
At our school to-day.

Additional Verses: Let's all make some bread; paint a mural; write a story; sing a song.

Jean Warren

What We Did Today

Sung to: Mary Had a Little Lamb

C
At our school we played today,

G7   C
Played today, played today.

At our school we played today.

G7   C
It was lots of fun.

C
At our school we read today,

G7   C
Read today, read today.

At our school we read today.

G7   C
It was lots of fun.

Additional Verses: At our school we painted today; cooked today; counted today; danced today.

Jean Warren

Learn  Sign

School

With left hand palm up and right hand palm down, clap right hand down on left hand twice.

I Like to Go to School

Sung to: The Farmer in the Dell

D
I like to go to school.

I like to go to school.

Our school is such a happy place,

A7   D
I like to go to school.

Additional Verses: I like to look at books; I like
to build with blocks; I like to listen to stories; I
like to draw and paint; I like to sing new
songs; I like to play with friends.

Betty Ruth Baker and Ann-Marie Donovan
Waco, TX   Framingham, MA

A Special Place

Sung to: Twinkle, Twinkle, Little Star

C   F   C
Letters, numbers, shapes, and rules:

G7   C   G7   C
These are things we learn at school.

     G7   C   G7
How to share and how to play,

C   G7   C   G7
How to have fun every day.

C   F   C
Going to school is so much fun,

     G7   C   G7   C
A special place for every-one.

Margery A. Kranyik
Hyde Park, MA

School

Sung to: Twinkle, Twinkle, Little Star

C   F   C
School will teach me how to share,

G7   C   G7   C
How to tell a friend I care.

               G7   C   G7
School will help me spell my name,

C   G7   C   G7
Help me learn to play a game.

C   F   C
School is where I like to be,

G7   C   G7   C
With my teachers helping me.

Margery A. Kranyik
Hyde Park, MA

All in a Day at School

Sung to: The Wheels on the Bus

     C
The children at the school

Come to work and play,
(Skip in a circle.)

G7   C
Work and play, work and play.

The children at the school

Come to work and play,

G7   C
Every day at school.

Continue with similar verses such as these:
The doors at the school go open and shut; The
children at the school like to build with blocks;
The swings at the school go back and forth.

Jan Miller
Gatesville, TX

At School

Sung to: Jimmy Crack Corn

F   C7
Coming to school every day,

                    F
Coming to school every day,

                  Bb
Coming to school every day

C7   F
Helps us as we grow.

F   C7
Playing at school every day,

                 F
Playing at school every day,

              Bb
Playing at school every day

C7   F
Helps us as we grow.

Additional Verses: Learning at school every day; Sharing at school every day.

Margery A. Kranyik
Hyde Park, MA

Our Teachers Show the Way

Sung to: The Farmer in the Dell

    D
At school we laugh and play.

It's fun to learn all day.

Create, explore, and so much more!

  A7   D
Our teachers show the way.

Shannon Shorey
Orlando, FL

At My School

Sung to: London Bridge

  C
I like to paint and build with blocks,

G   C
Build with blocks, build with blocks.

I like to paint and build with blocks,

G   C
At my scho-ol.

Additional Verses:
I like to sing and model clay.
I like to ride the trikes and swing.

Barb Robinson
Huntington Beach, CA

We Have Fun ✓

Sung to: Frere Jacques

C
We have fun. We have fun

At our school, at our school.

We like to play with blocks.

We like to play with blocks,

At our school, at our school.

Additional Verses: We like to read our books; play with clay; climb and swing; cut and paste.

Jean Warren

All About School

I'd Like to Meet You

Sung to: Skip to My Lou

C
I'd like to meet you; what is your name?

G7
I'd like to meet you; what is your name?

C
I'd like to meet you; what is your name?

G7   C
I like making friends.

> Jean Warren

What Is Your Name?

Sung to: Frere Jacques

C
What is your name? What is your name?

Tell us, please. Tell us, please.

We would like to meet you.

We would like to meet you.

What's your name? What's your name?

> Betty Silkunas
> Lansdale, PA

Who Are You?

Sung to: The Mulberry Bush

D
Tell me, tell me, tell me, do.

A7
Tell me, do, who are you?

D
Let's roll the ball and find out who.
(Roll the ball to one child.)

A7   D
What, oh, what is your name?
(Child says name.)

Sit on the floor in a circle and sing the song for each of your children.

> Lisa Feeney
> Pawling, NY

I'm Very Glad to
Meet You

Sung to: Skip to My Lou

F
I am Teddy. What is your name?
(First child gives name.)

C7
I am Teddy. What is your name?
(Next child gives name.)

F
I am Teddy. What is your name?
(Next child gives name.)

C7   F
I'm very glad to meet you.

Using a teddy bear as a puppet, continue singing the song until each child has had a turn.

> Laura Egge
> Lake Oswego, OR

Learn 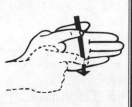 Sign

What

Point index finger of right hand and move it over extended fingers of left hand.

I'd Like to Know You Better

Sung to: The Little White Duck

C7   F   C7
What is your name? Is it Bob or Mary?

                                   F
What is your name? Is it Sue or Larry?

 B♭   F
I spent all day wondering what to say,

 G7   C7
In case you happened to come my way.

      F
Oh, what is your name? I'd like to know you
    C7
    better.

C   C7   F
What is your name?

    Jean Warren

Learn  Sign

Is

With right hand, make "I" handshape, touch small finger on mouth and move straight out.

Learn 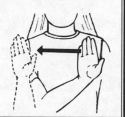 Sign

Your

Palm out, opened right hand moves across chest from left to right.

Learn  Sign

Name

Rest first two fingers of right hand on first two fingers of left hand, palms facing each other.

1-57029-521-2 *Piggyback Songs—School Days*

Learn 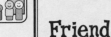 Sign

Friend

Interlock right and left index fingers, then separate hands and interlock again in opposite positions.

It's Fun to Get to Know You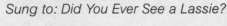

Sung to: Did You Ever See a Lassie?

  F
It's fun to get to know you,

  C7   F
To know you, to know you.

It's fun to get to know you

C7   F
And be your friend—

  C7   F
To play with, to work with,

  C7   F
To have so much fun with.

It's fun to get to know you

C7   F
And be your friend.

Patricia Coyne
Mansfield, MA

Have You Met a Friend of Mine?

Sung to: The Muffin Man

F
Have you met a friend of mine,

  G7   C
A friend of mine, a friend of mine?

F
Have you met a friend of mine?

G   C   F
Her name is Joanie.

Substitute one of your children's names for the name Joanie.

Julie Israel
Ypsilanti, MI

Hello, New Friend

Sung to: Frere Jacques

C
My name is Ben. My name is Ben.
(Child points to self as the group sing his name.)

What is yours? What is yours?
(Child points to another child. That child says his or her name.)

How are you today, Sue?

Very well, I thank you.

Hello, new friend. Hello, new friend.

Substitute the names of your children for the names Ben *and* Sue.

Susan Miller
Kutztown, PA

  12 1-57029-521-2 *Piggyback Songs—School Days*

What Is Your Last Name?

Sung to: The Little White Duck

F   C7
¿Cual es tu apel-lido?

            F
What is your last name?

          C7
¿Cual es tu apel-lido?

   F
It is Brown.

Point to one of your children and have him or her substitute his or her last name for Brown.

Sonya Kranwinkel

Spanish Pronunciation

Kwahl ehs too ah-pay-YEE-doh?
What is your last name?
Kwahl ehs too ah-pay-YEE-doh?
It is Brown.

English Translation

What is your last name?
What is your last name?
What is your last name?
It is Brown.

The Name Game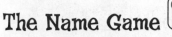

Sung to: The Muffin Man

F
Welcome, welcome, all my friends.

   G7   C7
We'll learn your name through this game.

F
Stand up, Nick, it is your turn.

G7   C7   F
Take a block, and then return.

Place one block for each child in a pile. Have the children sit in a circle around the blocks. Sing a verse for one of your children. Have the child named stand up, take one of the blocks and return to his or her place. Repeat until each child has had a turn.

Susan M. Paprocki
Northbrook, IL

13

1-57029-521-2 Piggyback Songs—School Days

Getting Acquainted—Names

Who Are You?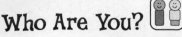
Sung to: Twinkle, Twinkle, Little Star

C   F   C
I am Betsy, who are you?
(Points to another child.)

G7   C   G7   C
I am Kenny, how about you?
(Chooses new child.)

       G7   C   G7
I am Annie, who are you?
(Points to another child.)

C   G7   C   G7
I am Jason, how about you?
(Chooses new child.)

C   F   C
I am Kathy, who are you?
(Points to another child.)

G7   C   G7   C
I am Peter, how about you?

Substitute the names of your children for the names in the song. Repeat the song until each child has had a chance to introduce him or herself.

Bev Qualheim
Marquette, MI

Who's at School?
Sung to: Old MacDonald Had a Farm

F   Bb   F
Mrs. Williams has a class.

  C7 F
E-I-E-I-O.

                    Bb   F
And in her class she has some children.

   C7 F
E-I-E-I-O.

With a Kevin here and a Rachel there,

Here a Daniel, there a Katie,

Over here a Nick and Tia.

              Bb   F
Mrs. Williams has a class.

  C7 F
E-I-E-I-O.

Substitute your name for Mrs. Williams *and the names of your children for those in the song. Continue singing until all your children have been named.*

Laura Egge
Lake Oswego, OR

Shake Your Hand

Sung to: Old MacDonald Had a Farm

F   Bb   F
He would like to shake your hand,

                 C7 F
And say hel-lo to you.

               Bb   F
He will tell you his name's Kelly.

             C7   F
Now tell him your name, too.
(Child says name.)

Hello, Susie; hello, Susie; hello, hello, hello,
   Susie.

               Bb   F
He would like to shake your hand
(Shake hands.)

               C7 F
And say hel-lo to you.

Substitute the names of your children for the names Kelly *and* Susie. *Continue singing the song until each child has had a chance to shake someone's hand.*

Patricia Coyne
Mansfield, MA

Welcome Song

Sung to: Oh, My Darling Clementine

         F
Little Reid, little Reid,

                      C7
Little Reid is new to-day.

                            F
We are glad you've joined our classroom,

         C7   F
And we hope that you will stay.

Substitute the name of your new student for the name Reid, *and the name of your group for the word* classroom.

Judy Hall
Wytheville, VA

Getting Acquainted

Sung to: Frere Jacques

C
Who is hiding? Who is hiding?

Who are you? Who are you?

We think it is Libby.

We think it is Libby.

Is that true? Is that true?

Have each child in turn cover his or her face. Then sing the song for the child, substituting his or her name for Libby.

Linda Filemyr
Baltimore, MD

1-57029-521-2 *Piggyback Songs—School Days*

To Our School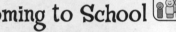

Sung to: Over the River and Through the Woods

C
Over the bridges and through the streets,

     F   G7   C
It's to our school we go.

     F   C
The drivers know the way to go

     G7   C
As they drive us safe and slow.

C
Over the bridges and through the streets,

     F   G7   C
In rain and sleet and snow.

     F   C
They drive with care; they get us there,

     G7   C
As over the streets we go.

Judy Hall
Wytheville, VA

Coming to School

Sung to: The Mulberry Bush

D
This is the way we come to school,

A7
Come to school, come to school.

D
This is the way we come to school,

A7   D
Early in the morning.

D
Some of us like to walk to school,

A7
Walk to school, walk to school.

D
Some of us like to walk to school,

A7   D
Early in the morning.

D
Some of us take the bus to school,

A7
Bus to school, bus to school.

D
Some of us take the bus to school,

A7   D
Early in the morning.

D
Some of us ride in the family car,

A7
Family car, family car.

D
Some of us ride in the family car,

A7   D
Early in the morning.

Continue with similar verses about ways your children come to school.

Margery A. Kranyik
Hyde Park, MA

1-57029-521-2 *Piggyback Songs—School Days*

Down at the Bus Stop

Sung to: Down by the Station

C
Down at the bus stop

G   C
Early in the morning,

See all the children,

G   C
Everyone we know,

Waiting for the school bus,

G   C
Safely on the sidewalk.

Honk-honk, beep-beep,

G   C
Off we go.

> Judy Hall
> Wytheville, VA

Waiting for the Bus

Sung to: Frere Jacques

C
I am waiting; I am waiting

For the bus, for the bus.

When will it get here?

Hopefully it is near.

Here it comes; here it comes.

> Lindsay Hall
> Wytheville, VA

The Children on the Bus

Sung to: The Wheels on the Bus

       F
The children on the bus sit nice and quiet,

C   F
Nice and quiet, nice and quiet.

The children on the bus sit nice and quiet

C   F
When we take a ride.

       F
The children on the bus look out the window,

C   F
Out the window, out the window.

The children on the bus look out the window

C   F
When we take a ride.

       F
The children on the bus stay in their seats,

C   F
In their seats, in their seats.

The children on the bus stay in their seats

C   F
When we take a ride.

> Cindy Dingwall
> Palatine, IL

I Like to Ride

Sung to: My Bonnie Lies Over the Ocean

```
        C       F      C
Me gusta ir en bus,

  C     D7      G
I like to ride the bus.

        C       F          C
Me gusta montar mi triciclo,

  F       G       C
I like to ride my trike.


        C       F
Me gusta ir en carro,

  G               C
I like to ride in the car.

C             F
I also like to walk,

G                 C
Me gusta cami-nar.
```

Sonya Kranwinkel

Spanish Pronunciation

May GOO-stah eer en boos.
I like to ride the bus.
May GOO-stah mohn-TAHR mee tree-SEE-kloh.
I like to ride my trike.

May GOO-stah eer en CAH-rroh.
I like to ride in the car.
I also like to walk.
May GOO-stah kah-mee-NAHR.

English Translation

I like to ride the bus.
I like to ride the bus.
I like to ride my trike.
I like to ride my trike.

I like to ride in the car.
I like to ride in the car.
I also like to walk.
I like to walk.

Beginning of the Day—Bus Ride

School's Begun

Sung to: Twinkle, Twinkle, Little Star

C   F   C
Ding-dong, ding-dong, school's be-gun.

G7   C   G7   C
Ding-dong, ding-dong, let's have fun.

C   G7   C   G7
Learning our numbers, colors, too,

C   G7   C   G7
And our letters, just for you.

C   F   C
Ding-dong, ding-dong, school's be-gun.

G7   C   G7   C
Ding-dong, ding-dong, let's have fun.

Judy Hall
Wytheville, VA

Early Morning Schoolyard

Sung to: Down by the Station

C   G   C
Down by the schoolyard, early in the morning,

                                  G   C
See the yellow buses, lining up so well,

                                     G
Dropping off the children, going to their
      C
      classrooms.

                               G   C
Bong-bong, ding-dong, there's the bell.

Judy Hall
Wytheville, VA

Morning Greeting

Sung to: Down by the Station

G   D7   G
Outside the schoolroom early in the morning,

                         D7
See the happy children, standing straight and
    G
    tall.

                         D7
Now we see the teacher greet the waiting
    children,

            D7   G
"Come in, children, one and all!"

Ellen Javernick
Loveland, CO

1-57029-521-2 *Piggyback Songs—School Days*

Beginning of the Day—Arrival

How Are You This Morning?

Sung to: Frere Jacques

C
Good morning. Good morning.

How are you? How are you?

It sure is good to see you.

It sure is good to see you.

We'll have fun. We'll have fun.

> Cindy Dingwall
> Palatine, IL

Good Morning

Sung to: Happy Birthday

F   C
Buenos días a ti.

          F
Buenos días a ti.

               B♭
Buenos días, Juan-ito.

     F   C F
Buenos días, a ti.

> New Eton School Staff

Spanish Pronunciation

BWEH-nohs DEE-ahs ah tee.
BWEH-nohs DEE-ahs ah tee.
BWEH-nohs DEE-ahs, Hwah-NEE-toe.
BWEH-nohs DEE-ahs ah tee.

English Translation

Good morning to you.
Good morning to you.
Good morning, Johnny.
Good morning to you.

Good morning to you.

Buenos días a ti.

1-57029-521-2 *Piggyback Songs—School Days*

I'm So Glad You Came

Sung to: London Bridge

C
Welcome to school today,

G   C
School today, school today.

Welcome to school today,

G   C
I'm so glad you came.

C
My name is Mrs. Brown,

G   C
Mrs. Brown, Mrs. Brown.

My name is Mrs. Brown,

G   C
I'm so glad you came.

Substitute your name for the name Mrs. Brown.

Karen Brown
Siloam Springs, AR

Welcome

Sung to: Happy Birthday

     F   C
We welcome you here,

         F
We welcome you here.

            B♭
We welcome every-body,

F   C   F
We welcome you here.

Judy Hall
Wytheville, VA

We Welcome You

Sung to: Mary Had a Little Lamb

   C
We welcome you to school today,

G7   C
School today, school today.

We welcome you to school today.

G7   C
Please come in and play.

        C
We're glad to have you here today,

G7   C
Here today, here today.

We're glad to have you here today.

  G7   C
Yes, it's a special day!

Deborah A. Roessel
Flemington, NJ

Learn Sign

Welcome

Start with open right hand in front of body, then bring it down in an arc that ends with palm up at left side of chest.

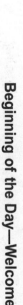

Beginning of the Day—Welcome

Let's Work and Play

Sung to: Sailing, Sailing

C
Welcome, children,

    F   C
We're glad you're here to-day.

    G7   C
We're going to work; we're going to play,

D   G7
All along the way.

C
Welcome, children,

F   C
Stay with us a while.

    G7   C
I'm sure you'll have a special day

    D   G   C
And leave here with a smile.

    Judy Hall
    Wytheville, VA

Welcome, Friends

Sung to: Goodnight, Ladies

F
Welcome, new friends.

        C
Welcome, old friends.

F   B♭
Welcome, welcome.

    F   C   F
We're glad to see you all!

F
You are special.

        C
I am special.

F   B♭
We are so glad

    F   C   F
That we have such good pals!

    Diane Thom
    Maple Valley, WA

Welcome to Our Group

Sung to: Row, Row, Row Your Boat

C
Welcome to our group.

We're glad you're here today.

We know you'll have a lot of fun

While you learn and play!

    Kathy McCullough
    St. Charles, IL

Greeting Song

Sung to: The Farmer in the Dell

Teacher:

    D
I'm glad you came today,

I'm glad you came today.

Hello, hello to everyone,
(Wave hello.)

    A7   D
I'm glad you came to-day.

Children:

    D
We're glad we came today,

We're glad we came today.

Hello, hello to everyone,
(Wave hello.)

    A7   D
We're glad we came to-day.

All:

    D
We'll work and play today,

We'll work and play today.

Hello, hello to everyone,
(Wave hello.)

    A7   D
We'll work and play to-day.

    Betty Ruth Baker
    Waco, TX

H-E-L-L-O

Sung to: Bingo

F   Bb   F
When you greet some-one you know,

             C   F
Hello is what you say-o.

    Bb   C   F   Bb
H-E-L-L-O, H-E-L-L-O, H-E-L-L-O,

    C   F
Hel-lo is what you say-o.

    Janice Bodenstedt
    Jackson, MI

Hello, Children

Sung to: Goodnight, Ladies

C   G7
Hello, children; hello, children,

C   F   C   G7   C
Hello, children; I'm glad you're here to-day.

    Judy Hall
    Wytheville, VA

 ## Learn Sign

Hello

Start open right hand, palm out, by face, then wave back and forth.

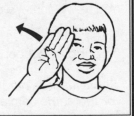

1-57029-521-2 Piggyback Songs—School Days

Hello

Sung to: Frere Jacques

C
Hello, Shelley. Hello, Shelley.

How are you? How are you?

We're so glad to have you,

We're so glad to have you.

Here at school, here at school.

Substitute the name of one of your children for the name Shelley, *and the name of your group for the word* school.

Linda Ferguson
Olympia, WA

Hello Song

Sung to: Three Blind Mice

C   G7 C   G7 C
Hel-lo, Jamie. Hel-lo, Jamie.

   G7 C   G7 C
How are you? How are you?

              G7   C
We're glad you're here to laugh and play.

              G7   C
We hope you'll have some fun today.

              G7   C
You're welcome, welcome everyday

   G7   C
To our play-school.

Substitute the name of one of your children for the name Jamie, *and the name of your group for the word* playschool.

Bev Qualheim
Marquette, MI

Good Morning Song

Sung to: Skip to My Lou

C
Hello, how are you?

G7
Hello, how are you?

C
Hello, how are you?

G7   C
How are you to-day?

C
I'm fine, how about you?

G7
I'm fine, how about you?

C
I'm fine, how about you?

G7   C
I'm just fine to-day.

C
Turn to you neighbor and shake their hand.
(as above, 3 times)

G7   C
How are you to-day?

C
It's good to see you back again.
(as above, 3 times)

   G7   C
We hope you're feeling fine.

Joanne Cameron
Santa Maria, CA

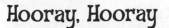

Who Is Here Today?

Sung to: Twinkle, Twinkle, Little Star

C   F   C
Let's see who is here to-day,

G7   C   G7   C
Who has come to join our play?

       G7   C   G7
Every-one sit close at hand,

C   G7   C   G7
Say your name, then you can stand.

C   F   C
Let's see who is here to-day,

G7   C   G7   C
Who has come to join our play?

Ellen Bedford
Bridgeport, CT

Song for Taking Attendance

Sung to: Twinkle, Twinkle, Little Star

C   F   C
(Mary) came to school to-day.

G7   C   G7   C
We're so glad, we'll shout, "Hoo-ray!"

Roberta Mohr
Bluffton, OH

Hooray, Hooray

Sung to: Twinkle, Twinkle, Little Star

C   F   C
Carmen's here, hoo-ray, hoo-ray!

G7   C   G7   C
I wonder what she'll do to-day.

C   G7   C   G7
Paint a picture? Play with toys?

C   G7   C   G7
Sing with other girls and boys?

C   F   C
Carmen's here, hoo-ray, hoo-ray!

G7   C   G7   C
I wonder what she'll do to-day.

Sing the song for each of your children, substituting the child's name for Carmen *and something that the child might like to do for* paint a picture.

Laura Egge
Lake Oswego, OR

1-57029-521-2 Piggyback Songs—School Days

We're So Glad

Sung to: If You're Happy and You Know It

      G   C
We're so glad you've come to school to-day.

                                  G
We're so glad you've come to school to-day.

C
Kristy, won't you stand,

      G
And shake Linda's hand.

      D   G
Now everybody clap and say, "O-lé!" (Olé!)

      G   D
We're so glad you've come to school to-day.

                                  G
We're so glad you've come to school to-day.

C
Elizabeth stamp your feet,

      G
And Eric smile so sweet.

      D   G
Now everybody clap and say, "O-lé!" (Olé!)

        G   D
We're so glad you've come to school to-day.

                                  G
We're so glad you've come to school to-day.

C
Susan take a bow,

G
And Kevin, blink right now.

      D   G
Now everybody stand and say, "O-lé!" (Olé!)

      G   D
We're so glad you've come to school to-day.

                                  G
We're so glad you've come to school to-day.

C
Eileen hop about,

      G
And David give a shout.

      D   G
Now everybody clap and say, "O-lé!" (Olé!)

      G   D
We're so glad you've come to school to-day.

                                  G
We're so glad you've come to school to-day.

C
Kathleen touch your chin,

      G
And Dorothy, show a grin.

      D   G
Now everybody clap and say, "O-lé!" (Olé!)

Substitute the names of your children for the names in the song. Have the children act out the motions as their names are called.

Marie Wheeler
Tacoma, WA

1-57029-521-2 *Piggyback Songs—School Days*

Beginning of the Day

Glad to See You

Sung to: Frere Jacques

Teacher:

C
I'm Ms. Baker. I'm Ms. Baker.

That's my name. That's my name.

Glad to see you here.

Glad to see you here.

What's your name? What's your name?

Child:

C
I am Bobby. I am Bobby.

That's my name. That's my name.

I am glad to be here. I am glad to be here

At school today, at school today.

*Substitute your name and the name of one of
your children for the names* Ms. Baker *and* Bobby.

Betty Ruth Baker
Waco, TX

Welcome Song

Sung to: Mary Had a Little Lamb

C
Cody came to school today,

G7   C
School today, school today.

Cody came to school today.

G7   C
We're so glad he's here.

C
Let's all clap for Cody now,
(Clap.)

G7   C
Cody now, Cody now.

Let's all clap for Cody now

  G7   C
And give a great big cheer.
(Give a cheer.)

Elizabeth McKinnon

Here We Are Together

Sung to: In and Out the Window

  F   C
So here we are to-gether,

  C   F
So here we are to-gether,

  F   C
So here we are to-gether,

C   F
Let's all say, "Hel-lo."

  F   C
There's Ann and John and Mary,

  C   F
There's Tom and Mike and Jenny,

  F   C
There's Chris and Bill and Matthew,

C   F
We're so glad you're here.

*Substitute the names of students in your class
for the names in this song.*

Barb Robinson
Huntington Beach, CA

1-57029-521-2 Piggyback Songs—School Days

Beginning of the Day

Start the Day with a Smile
Sung to: The Mulberry Bush

C
This is the way we start the day,

G
Start the day, start the day.

C
This is the way we start the day,

  G   C
So early in the morning.

C
First we smile and shake a hand,

G
Shake a hand, shake a hand.

C
First we smile and shake a hand,

  G   C
So early in the morning.

C
Then we sit down quietly,

G
Quietly, quietly.

C
Then we sit down quietly,

  G   C
So early in the morning.

    C
We listen very carefully,

G
Carefully, carefully.

   C
We listen very carefully,

  G   C
So early in the morning.

    Rita Galloway
    Harlington, TX

Starting the Day
Sung to: Mary Had a Little Lamb

C
Merrily we start the day,

G   C
Start the day, start the day.

Merrily we start the day,

G   C
All of us at school.

    Judy Hall
    Wytheville, VA

A Happy Start
Sung to: Skip to My Lou

      F
Let's start the day in a happy way;

      C7
Let's start the day in happy way;

      F
Let's start the day in a happy way;

C7   F
Let's get ready to learn and play.

    Tami Hall
    Owasso, OK

Exciting Day
Sung to: Row, Row, Row Your Boat

   C
It's time, time, time to start,

Time to start the day.

We will finish all our work,

And then we'll stop and play.

    Kristina Carle and Nanette Belice
    Kensington, MD

We Have Rules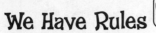

Sung to: Three Blind Mice

C G7 C   G7   C
We have rules; we have rules

   G7 C   G7 C
In our school; in our school.

       G7   C
We use inside voices and walking feet.

       G7   C
We don't touch or bother the friends we meet.

       G7   C
And when we're eating, we stay in our seats,

       G7 C
'Cause we have rules.

Priscilla M. Starrett
Warren, PA

Singing Praises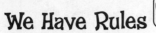

Sung to: Frere Jacques

C
I see David. I see David

Raising his hand, raising his hand.

That is what we all should do,

That is what we all should do.

Thank you, David. Thank you, David.

*Substitute the name of one of your children
for* David *and an appropriate phrase, such as*
sitting on the rug *or* sharing the blocks, *for*
raising his hand.

Laura Egge
Lake Oswego, OR

Walking Feet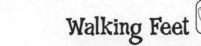

Sung to: Frere Jacques

C
Walking feet, walking feet—

See them slide. See them glide.

They never run inside the room.

They never run inside the room,

Just outside, just outside.

Laura Egge
Lake Oswego, OR

1-57029-521-2 *Piggyback Songs—School Days*

Guidance

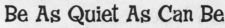

Quiet Voices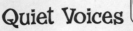

Sung to: Frere Jacques

C
Quiet voices, quiet voices

In the room, in the room.

Noisy voices outside,

Quiet voices inside,

In the room, in the room.

> Laura Egge
> Lake Oswego, OR

Shh! It's Too Noisy

Sung to: Pop! Goes the Weasel

D   A7   D
All a-round our room today,

          A7   D
The children were so noisy.

            A7   D
They couldn't hear the teacher say,

G   A7   D
"Shh! It's too noisy!"

> Laura Egge
> Lake Oswego, OR

Be As Quiet As Can Be

Sung to: Oh, My Darling Clementine

            F
Let's sit down; let's sit down;

                    C7
Let's sit down so quiet-ly.

                    F
Let's sit down; let's sit down;

    C7   F
Be as quiet as can be!

Additional Verses: Let's stand up; Let's line up.

> Lois Putnam
> Pilot Mt., NC

Getting Attention

Sung to: If You're Happy and You Know It

F   C
If you can hear my voice, touch your nose.

                            F
If you can hear my voice, touch your nose.

Bb
If you're not making noise,

     F
You can surely hear my voice.

C   F
If you can hear my voice, touch your nose.

Repeat, each time substituting a different phrase, such as raise your hand *or* tap your toe, *for* touch your nose.

Laura Egge
Lake Oswego, OR

Please Be Quiet

Sung to: Oh, My Darling Clementine

               F
Please be quiet, please be quiet,

                  C7
Please be quiet just now.

                    F
Sh-sh-sh-sh-, sh-sh-sh-sh,
(Put finger to lips.)

        C7   F
Please be quiet just now.

Lois Putnam
Pilot Mt., NC

A Quiet Voice

Sung to: I've Been Working on the Railroad

G
There's a quiet voice inside me,

C   G
Soft as it can be.

There's a quiet voice inside me.

  A7   D7
It's hushed and whisper-y.

                 G
I will use it in the school room,

   C   B
The hall and librar-y.

C   G
And I know that every-body

  D7   G
Will be so proud of me!

Margo S. Miller
Westerville, OH

1-57029-521-2 *Piggyback Songs—School Days*

Guidance—Quiet Voices

Listen, Everyone

Sung to: Twinkle, Twinkle, Little Star

C   F   C
Listen, listen, every-one.

G7   C   G7   C
Now our playing time is done.

C   G7   C   G7
Let's sit down, and let's be quiet.

C   G7 C   G7
We can do it if we try it.

C   F   C
Listen, listen, every-one.

G7   C   G7   C
Now our playing time is done.

Substitute an appropriate time, such as
outdoor time *or* painting time, *for* playing time.

Laura Egge
Lake Oswego, OR

If Your Name Begins with "A"

Sung to: If You're Happy and You Know It

G   D
If your name begins with A, wash your hands.

                             G
If your name begins with A, wash your hands.

           C
If your name begins with A,

           G
If your name begins with A,

D   G
If your name begins with A, wash your hands.

Substitute other letters for the letter A *and*
names of other activities for wash your hands.

Betty Silkunas
Lansdale, PA

Transition Times

32

1-57029-521-2 *Piggyback Songs—School Days*

If You're Wearing Something Red

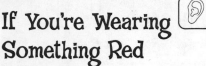

Sung to: If You're Happy and You Know It

       F   C
If you're wearing something red, get your coat.

                                   F
If you're wearing something red, get your coat.

       B♭
If you're wearing something red,

       F
If you're wearing something red,

       C   F
If you're wearing something red, get your coat.

Repeat, each time substituting the name of a different color for red *or an appropriate phrase, such as* you may go, *or* please wash up, *for* get your coat.

       Laura Egge
       Lake Oswego, OR

Transition Time

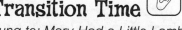

Sung to: Mary Had a Little Lamb

C
All the people wearing green,

G   C
Wearing green, wearing green.

All the people wearing green,

     G7   C
Stand by the door right now.

Substitute such characteristics as born in June; with brown hair, *etc., for* wearing green; *and the appropriate action for* stand by the door.

       Ellen Javernick
       Loveland, CO

Who May Go?

Sung to: London Bridge

C
If you wore a hat today,

G7   C
Hat today, hat today.

If you wore a hat today,

G7   C
You may go now.

Repeat, each time substituting the name of a different article of clothing for hat.

       Laura Egge
       Lake Oswego, OR

Stand in Line

Sung to: She'll Be Coming 'Round the Mountain

          F
If you're wearing tennis shoes, stand in line.

                                 C
If you're wearing tennis shoes, stand in line.

          F
If you're wearing tennis shoes,

       B♭
If you're wearing tennis shoes,

       F   C7   F
If you're wearing tennis shoes, stand in line.

Substitute other clothing names for the words tennis shoes *until all of the children are in line.*

       Betty Silkunas
       Lansdale, PA

1-57029-521-2 *Piggyback Songs—School Days*

Move So Fine in Line

Sung to: Hokey-Pokey

C
We keep our eyes straight ahead,

We keep our hands at our sides,

We keep our feet so, so quiet,

     G
As right out the door we glide.

We move so fine in line,

No one turns themselves around—

       C
That's what it's all a-bout!

    Betty Silkunas
    Lansdale, PA

Come with Me

Sung to: Row, Row, Row Your Boat

C
Come, come, come with me;

Time to go inside.

Line up straight and quietly,

Then please follow me.

    Cindy Dingwall
    Palatine, IL

Line Up

Sung to: Skip to My Lou

F
Line up, line up, get in line.

C7
Line up, line up, get in line.

F
Line up, line up, get in line.

C7   F
We're going to go to lunch.

*Substitute the name of your next activity for
the word* lunch.

    Sue Brown
    Louisville, KY

Transition Times—Line Up

34

1-57029-521-2 *Piggyback Songs—School Days*

Who Wants to Go?

Sung to: Jimmy Crack Corn

F   C7
Who wants to go and play outside?
(Adult sings.)

                F
We want to go and play outside!
(Everyone sings.)

               B♭
Who wants to go and play outside?
(Adult sings.)

C7   F
We all want to go!
(Everyone sings.)

Substitute an appropriate phrase, such as go
and stand in line *or* go to the library, *for* go
and play outside.

Laura Egge
Lake Oswego, OR

Walk, Walk

Sung to: Skip to My Lou

F
Walk, walk, walk your feet.

C7
Walk, walk, walk your feet.

F
Walk, walk, walk your feet.

C7   F
Walk right to the sandbox.

*Substitute the name of an appropriate
destination, such as* snack table *or*
playground, *for* sandbox.

Gayle Bittinger

Now It's Time

Sung to: The Mulberry Bush

D
Now it's time to go outside,

A7
Go outside, go outside.

D
Now it's time to go outside,

   A7   D
So early in the morning.

Substitute an appropriate phrase, such as sit
on the rug, eat our snack, *or* stand in line, *for*
go outside.

Laura Egge
Lake Oswego, OR

Ready to Go Outside

Sung to: When the Saints Go Marching In

          C
Oh, when we all, oh, when we all,

                 G7
Oh, when we all are standing still,

        C   F
We will be ready to go out-side,

        C   G7 C
When we all are stand-ing still.

Ellen Javernick
Loveland, CO

35

Let's All Go to the Library

Sung to: Ten Little Indians

C
Let's all go to the biblioteca.

G7
Let's all go to the biblioteca.

C
Let's all go to the biblioteca,

   G7   C
So we can get some books!

Additional Verses:
Parque/So we can run and play!
Escuela/So we can learn and draw!
Dentista/So she can check our teeth!
Campo de juego/So we can climb and play!
Casa de Abuela/So we can visit her!
Casa de Abuelo/So we can visit him!
Jardin zoológico/So we can see the animals!
Médica/So she can check our health!
Mercado/So we can buy some food!

Vicki Shannon

Spanish Pronunciation

Let's all go to the bee-blee-oh-TAY-kah.
Let's all go to the bee-blee-oh-TAY-kah.
Let's all go to the bee-blee-oh-TAY-kah,
So we can get some books!

Additional Verses:
PAHR-kay/So we can run and play!
Es-KUAY-lah/So we can learn and draw!
Dehn-TEE-stah/So she can check our teeth!
CAHM-poh day HUAY-goh/So we can climb
   and play!
KAH-sah day ah-BWAY-lah/So we can visit her!
KAH-sah day ah-BWAY-loh/So we can visit him!
Hahr-DEEN soo-oh-LOH-hee-koh/So we can
   see the animals!
MEH-dee-coh/So she can check our health!
Mehr-KAH-doh/So we can buy some food!

English Translation

Let's all go to the library.
Let's all go to the library.
Let's all go to the library,
So we can get some books!

Additional Verses:
Park/So we can run and play!
School/So we can learn and draw!
Dentist/So she can check our teeth!
Playground/So we can climb and play!
Grandma's house/So we can visit her!
Grandpa's house/So we can visit him!
Zoo/So we can see the animals!
Doctor/So she can check our health!
Market/So we can buy some food.

Transition Times—Going Somewhere

1-57029-521-2 *Piggyback Songs—School Days*

Guess What It's Time to Do

Sung to: Oh, Dear, What Can the Matter Be?

C
Oh, my, guess what it's time to do.

G7
Oh, my, guess what it's time to do.

C
Oh, my, guess what it's time to do.

G7   C
Come over here and find out.

> Cindy Dingwall
> Palatine, IL

Who Wants To?

Sung to: London Bridge

C
Who wants to do some painting now,

G7   C
Painting now, painting now?

Who wants to do some painting now?

G7   C
Who is ready?

Substitute an appropriate phrase, such as do
some cooking now, *or* play a game with me,
for do some painting now.

> Laura Egge
> Lake Oswego, OR

Away We Go

Sung to: The Farmer in the Dell

D
Playtime is here.

Playtime is here.

Heigh-ho and away we go,

A7   D
Playtime is here.

Substitute other special times such as snack
time, lunchtime, naptime, *etc., for* playtime.

> Jean Warren

Transition Times—Time for...

Are You Ready?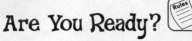

Sung to: Frere Jacques

C
Are you ready? Are you ready?
(Clap.)

Please sit down; please sit down.
(Sit down.)

Time to quiet down now. Time to quiet down
    now.
(Put finger on lips.)

Hands on laps, hands on laps.
(Place hands on lap.)

Ellen Javernick
Loveland, CO

We All Need to Sit Down

Sung to: Frere Jacques

C
Sit on the rug. Sit on the rug
(Sit on rug.)

Like we should, like we should.

We all need to sit down.

We all need to sit down.

Very good. Very good.

Substitute an appropriate word, such as floor
or chairs *for* rug.

Laura Egge
Lake Oswego, OR

It's Time

Sung to: The Farmer in the Dell

D
It's time to come to group,

It's time to come to group.

Come on over; find a seat.

        A7   D
It's time to come to group.

Sue Brown
Louisville, KY

Come Around

Sung to: Twinkle, Twinkle, Little Star

C   F   C
Joseph and Kelsey, come a-round.

G7   C G7   C
Peter and Ali, sit on the ground.

C   G7   C   G7
Abby and Tommy will sit next to you.

C   G7   C   G7
Emi, Billy, and Kim will, too.

C   F   C
Andrew, Andrew is the last one.

G7   C   G7   C
Now we're ready to have some fun!

*Substitute the name of your children for those
in the song.*

Krista Alworth
Verona, NJ

Published by Totline Publications. Copyright protected.

1-57029-521-2 *Piggyback Songs—School Days*

Group Time

Circle Time

Sung to: London Bridge

C
See the circles on the floor,

G   C
On the floor, on the floor.

See the circles on the floor,

G   C
On the floor.

C
Find a circle and stand on one,

G   C
Stand on one, stand on one.

Find a circle and stand on one,

G   C
Stand on one.

C
Fold your legs and sit right down,

G   C
Sit right down, sit right down.

Fold your legs and sit right down,

G   C
Sit right down.

C
Let's all listen to the teacher,

G   C
To the teacher, to the teacher.

Let's all listen to the teacher,

G   C
It is circle time.

*Make circles on the floor in any arrangement
using construction paper, masking tape, etc.
As you sing the song, have the children follow
the directions.*

Lois Olson
Webster City, IA

Join Us in the Circle

Sung to: Yankee Doodle

C   G7
Join us in the circle, please,

C   G7
Find a special place.

C
Cross your legs,

    F
No wiggles, please,

G7   C
Show us your smiling face.

F
Join us in the circle, please,

C
Find a special place.

F
Cross your legs,

No wiggles, please,

    C   G7   C
Show us your smiling face.

Betty Silkunas
Lansdale, PA

Circle Time

Sung to: Twinkle, Twinkle, Little Star

C   F   C
Here's my ribbon, flat as can be.

   G7   C   G7   C
I'm going to give it some wiggles, you see.
(Hold up a piece of ribbon.)

C   G7   C   G7
Watch me wiggle it, oh, so high.

C   G7   C   G7
Watch me toss it up in the sky.
(Wiggle ribbon and toss it away.)

C   F   C
All my wiggles are gone from me.

   G7   C   G7   C
I gave them to my ribbon, as you can see.
(Sit quietly with hands folded.)

*Give each of your children a piece of ribbon
before singing the song.*

Patty Claycomb
Ventura, CA

If a Wiggle's in Your Leg

Sung to: If You're Happy and You Know It

      F   C
If a wiggle's in your leg, shake it out.
(Shake leg.)

                               F
If a wiggle's in your leg, shake it out.

     B♭   F
If you have a little wiggle, it will surely make
    you giggle.

     C   F
If a wiggle's in your leg, shake it out.

*Repeat, each time substituting the name of a
different body part for* leg.

Laura Egge
Lake Oswego, OR

Wiggles

Sung to: I'm a Little Teapot

C
Wiggles in my pockets—

F   C
Get them out!

G7   C
Wiggles in my socks—

  G7   C
I wiggle them out.

                        F   C
Wiggles and waggles and woggles and shouts,

                  F   G7   C
I'll waggle and woggle those wiggles right out!

Michele Triplett
Peoria, IL

Ready to Listen

Sung to: Twinkle, Twinkle, Little Star

C   F   C
Let your hands go clap, clap, clap.
(Clap hands.)

G7   C   G7   C
Let your fingers go snap, snap, snap.
(Snap fingers.)

C   G7   C   G7
Let your lips go up and down,
(Open and close mouth.)

C   G7   C   G7
But don't let them make a sound.
(Hold finger to lips.)

C   F   C
Fold your hands and close each eye.
(Fold hands and close eyes.)

G7   C   G7   C
Take a breath, then softly sigh.
(Breathe deeply and say, "Ahhh.")

Adapted Traditional

Group Time—Calm Down

Time for Stories

Sung to: Oh, My Darling Clementine

C
Time for stories, time for stories,

        G7
Time for stories to-day.

        C
Let's sit down. Let's be quiet.

   G7   C
Wonder what we'll hear to-day.

> Cindy Dingwall
> Palatine, IL

If You're Ready

Sung to: If You're Happy and You Know It

    G   D
If you're ready for a story, find a seat.

                G
If you're ready for a story, find a seat.

    C
If you're ready for a story,

       G
Check your hands and then your feet.

   D   G
If you're ready for a story, find a seat.

> Sue Brown
> Louisville, KY

I'm a Ready Listener

Sung to: I'm a Little Teapot

C   F   C
I'm a ready listener, read me a book,

G7   C   G7   C
Hands in my lap, at the teacher I look.

             F   C
When I get all ready, the teacher will say,

      F   G7   C
"This is the story that I have for you to-day."

> Tami Hall
> Owasso, OK

Published by Totline Publications. Copyright protected.

1-57029-521-2 *Piggyback Songs—School Days*

Story Time

Take a Look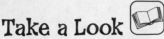

Sung to: If You're Happy and You Know It

 F   C
Take a look; take a look at my book.

 F   F
Take a look; take a look at my book.

 Bb
Turn the pages nice and slow.

 F
Look at pictures as you go.

 C   F
Take a look; take a look at my book.

> Elizabeth McKinnon

A Story

Sung to: Mary Had a Little Lamb

C
Would you like to hear a story,

G7   C
Hear a story, hear a story?

Would you like to hear a story?

G7   C
If so, sit with me.

> Angela Metzendorf
> Kinsman, OH

Hush Little Children

Sung to: Hush Little Baby

F
Hush, little children,

C7
Listen to me.

You'll like this story,

F
Just wait and see.

                    C7
And if you're very quiet,

My friends,

You'll have a turn to talk

        F
When the story ends.

> Laura Egge
> Lake Oswego, OR

Published by Totline Publications. Copyright protected.

1-57029-521-2 *Piggyback Songs—School Days*

It's Time for Show and Tell

Sung to: The Farmer in the Dell

   D
It's time for show and tell.

It's time for show and tell.

Hey, hey, it's lots of fun.

     A7   D
It's time for show and tell.

    Cindy Dingwall
    Palatine, IL

Special Things

Sung to: Jingle Bells

F
Show and tell, show and tell,

Show and tell today.

C7   F
Come and share your special things

   G7   C7
You brought along the way.

F
Show and tell, show and tell,

Show and tell today.

C7   F
Come and share your special things

   C7   F
You brought with you to-day.

    Judy Hall
    Wytheville, VA

Sharing Time

Sung to: Twinkle, Twinkle, Little Star

C   F   C
Won't you share your show and tell?

G7   C   G7   C
We will look and listen well.

            G7   C   G7
We know our turn will come soon,

C   G7   C G7
So we sing this little tune.

C   F   C
Won't you share your show and tell?

G7   C   G7   C
We will look and listen well.

    Betty Silkunas
    Lansdale, PA

1-57029-521-2 *Piggyback Songs—School Days*

Show and Tell

What's Inside?
Sung to: Mary Had a Little Lamb

C
Amy has a mystery bag,

G7   C
Mystery bag, mystery bag.

Amy has a mystery bag,

 G7   C
I wonder what's in-side.

C
She will give us all a clue,

G7   C
All a clue, all a clue.

She will give us all a clue,

   G7   C
To help guess what's in-side.

C
We will have to make a guess,

G7   C
Make a guess, make a guess.

We will have to make a guess,

   G7   C
To find out what's in-side.

*This is a group problem-solving activity. Have
the children bring their show-and-tell items in
bags. After you sing this song for one of your
children, have that child give clues about
what's in his or her bag while the other
children try to guess what it is.*

Ann-Marie Donovan
Framingham, MA

Sharing
Sung to: The Farmer in the Dell

   D
It's Jeff's turn to share.

It's Jeff's turn to share.

Let's look and see what Jeff has brought.

   A7   D
It's Jeff's turn to share.

*Substitute the name of one of your children
for the name Jeff.*

Paula Laughtland
Edmonds, WA

Show and Tell
Sung to: Mary Had a Little Lamb

C
It's Joey's turn for show and tell,

G7   C
Show and tell, show and tell.

It's Joey's turn for show and tell,

G7   C
Let's see what he brought.

*Substitute the name of one of your children
for the name Joey.*

Ann-Marie Donovan
Framingham, MA

Lots to See

Sung to: I'm a Little Teapot

C
Show and tell is great,

      F   C
There's lots to see.

   G7   C
It's fun for you,

     G7   C
And it's fun for me.

            F   C
Showing things to others is a joy,

        G7   C
For every little girl and boy.

> Susan Burbridge
> Beavercreek, OH

Ready to Share

Sung to: If You're Happy and You Know It

     G   D
If you're ready to share, clap your hands.

                  G
If you're ready to share, slap your knees.

     C
If you're ready to share,

  G
Then quiet you will be.

    D   G
If you're ready to share, fold your hands.

> Susan Peters
> Upland, CA

Let Us See It

Sung to: London Bridge

C
Eddie brought his show and tell,

G   C
Show and tell, show and tell.

Eddie brought his show and tell

G   C
With him today.

C
Take it out and show us now,

G   C
Show us now, show us now.

Take it out and show us now.

G   C
Let us see it.

Substitute the name of one of your children for the name Eddie.

> Judy Hall
> Wytheville, VA

Show and Tell

We All Like to Dance and Sing

Sung to: Mary Had a Little Lamb

C
We all like to dance and sing,

G   C
Dance and sing, dance and sing.

C
We all like to dance and sing,

G   C
Tra, la, la, la, la.

(Move body to tune and sing.)

Saundra Winnett
Fort Worth, TX

Sing, Sing, Sing

Sung to: Row, Row, Row Your Boat

C
Sing, sing, sing with me.

Sing out loud and clear,

To tell the people everywhere

That music time is here.

Mary Henthorne
LaCrescent, MN

The Ring

Sung to: The Mulberry Bush

D
All join hands and make a ring,

A
Make a ring, make a ring.

D
All join hands and make a ring,

A   D
While this song we sing.

D
Circle 'round in our ring,

A
In our ring, in our ring.

D
Circle 'round in our ring,

A   D
While this song we sing.

D
Clap our hands while we sing,

A
While we sing, while we sing.

D
Clap our hands while we sing,

A   D
In our circle ring.

Jean Warren

46

1-57029-521-2 *Piggyback Songs—School Days*

Music Time

M-U-S-I-C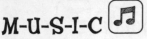

✓Sung to: Bingo

F   B♭   F
What makes us dance and clap and sing?

C   F
Yes, music is its name-o.

B♭   C   F   B♭   C
M-U-S-I-C, M-U-S-I-C, M-U-S-I-C,

F
Yes, music is its name-o.

Diane Thom
Maple Valley, WA

When the Band Comes Marching By

Sung to: When the Saints Go Marching In

C
Oh, when the band comes marching by,

G7
Oh, when the band comes marching by,

C   F
We will play and sing and be happy,

C   G7   C
When the band comes marching by.

Margery A. Kranyik
Hyde Park, MA

Our Marching Band ✓

Sung to: The Paw Paw Patch

F
One little, two little,

Three little instruments;

C7
Four little, five little,

Six little instruments;

F
Seven little, eight little,

Nine little instruments

C7
Playing loud and clear

F
In our marching band.

Have your children play instruments on each number as you sing the song.

Margery A. Kranyik
Hyde Park, MA

1-57029-521-2 *Piggyback Songs—School Days*

The More We Play Together

Sung to: Did You Ever See a Lassie?

F
The more we play together,

C7 F
To-gether, to-gether;

The more we play together,

C7   F
The happier we sound.

C7   F
The drums and the shakers,

C7   F
The sticks and the bells.

The more we play together,

C7 F
The happier we sound.

  Margery A. Kranyik
  Hyde Park, MA

Instrument Song

Sung to: Mary Had a Little Lamb

C
Triangles are playing,

G7 C
Playing, playing.

Triangles are playing

G   C
In our little band.

Additional Verses: Rhythm sticks are playing;
Jingle bells are playing; Tambourines are
playing; Little drums are playing; Shakers are
playing.

  Margery A. Kranyik
  Hyde Park, MA

Instrument Sounds

Sung to: The Mulberry Bush

D
This is the sound the little drums make,

A7
Little drums make, little drums make.

D
This is the sound the little drums make.

A7   D
Listen to them now.
(Beat drum three times.)

*Continue with similar verses, substituting
words such as* shakers, little bells *or* rhythm
sticks *for* little drums.

  Margery A. Kranyik
  Hyde Park, MA

I Play My Horn

Sung to: Up on the Housetop

F
I play my horn with a toot-toot-toot.

Bb   F   C7
Don't you think that it is cute?

F
I play my drum with a rum-pum-pum.

Bb   F   C F
Don't you think it's a happy drum?

Bb   Am   D7
Toot-toot-toot, rum-pum-pum.

Gm C7 F
Toot-toot-toot, rum-pum-pum.

          Bb F Bdim
All come along and join the fun,

F   Gm C7 F
While I play my horn and drum.

  Margo S. Miller
  Westerville, OH

Music Time—Instruments

48

If You Want to Have a Snack

Sung to: If You're Happy and You Know It

     F   C
If you want to have a snack, wash your hands.
(Pretend to wash hands.)

                                     F
If you want to have a snack, wash your hands.
(Pretend to wash hands.)

      B♭
Use a little soap and water,

     F
It's not really such a bother.

    C   F
If you want to have a snack, wash your hands.
(Pretend to wash hands.)

> Phyllis Martinelli
> Ooylestown, OH

Get Ready for Snacks

Sung to: Up on the Housetop

F
Let's get ready for snacks today,

B♭   F   C
See the clock; what does it say?

F
Time to put the toys away.

B♭   F   C   F
Hear your teacher, what does s/he say?

B♭   F
Wash your hands 'til they are clean,

C   F
All around and in between.

        F7   B♭ F B♭
Walk back quietly to your seats.

F   C   C7 F
Now you're ready for your good treats.

> Florence Dieckmann
> Roanoke, VA

We Love It So

Sung to: The Farmer In the Dell

     D
It's time to have a snack.

It's time to have a snack.

Yum, yum, we love it so;

    A7   D
It's time to have a snack.

     D
We'll have to wash our hands.

We'll have to wash our hands.

Yum, yum, we love it so;

    A7   D
We'll wash before we snack.

     D
We'll eat a healthful treat.

We'll eat a healthful treat.

Yum, yum, we love it so;

    A7   D
We'll eat a healthful treat.

> Cindy Dingwall
> Palatine, IL

Snack Time

Published by Totline Publications. Copyright protected.

1-57029-521-2 *Piggyback Songs—School Days*

Setting the Table

Sung to: The Mulberry Bush

D
This is the way we set the table,

A7
Set the table, set the table.

D
This is the way we set the table

A7   D
When it's time for a snack.

D
This is where we put the plates,

A7
Put the plates, put the plates.

D
This is where we put the plates

A7   D
When it's time for a snack.

Continue with similar verses, each time
substituting a different word, such as spoons
or bowls, *for* plates.

    Elizabeth McKinnon

Snack Time

Sung to: I'm a Little Teapot

C   F   C
It is time for us to have our snack,

G7   C   G7   C
Please sit down and hands in your lap.

              F   C
Wait 'til everyone is served their food

          F   G7   C
Then eat your snack; yum, yum, it's good.

    Patricia Coyne
    Mansfield, PA

Snack Song

Sung to: Down by the Station

F   C   F
Around our snack table, early in the morning,

F   C   F
We get lots of good things for our day.

F   C   F
Food we need to help us grow and play,

F   C   F
Chew, chew, crunch, crunch, down it goes!

    Sister Linda Kaman R.S.M.
    Pittsburgh, PA

Snack Attack

Sung to: Three Blind Mice

C   G7 C   G7 C
Snack at-tack, snack at-tack,

             G7   C   G7   C
A snack for us to eat—let's sit in our seats.

       G7   C
Peanuts or raisins or cheese would be great;

     G7   C
Even ba-nanas, I just can't wait.

     G7   C
Hurry, now, let's not be late.

     G7 C
Snack at-tack.

    Carol Kyger
    Hood River, OR

50

Time to Eat Our Snack

Sung to: She'll Be Coming 'Round the Mountain

      F
Oh, it's time to eat our snack now—

Yum, yum, yum!

Oh, it's time to eat our snack now—

C7
Yum, yum, yum!

      F
Oh, we're having milk today,

     Bb
And we think that that's okay.

     F   C7
Oh, it's time to eat our snack now—

F
Yum, yum, yum!

Substitute the name of a snack food you are serving for milk.

     Laura Egge
     Lake Oswego, OR

Eat Them Up

Sung to: Frere Jacques

C
Eat them up; eat them up,

Little Chad, little Chad.

Carrots and peas, very, very tasty!

Eat them up; eat them up.

Substitute the name of one of your children for Chad *and the foods he or she is eating for* carrots and peas.

     Michelle Monoc
     Kent, OH

I Like to Eat

Sung to: Skip to My Lou

F
I like to eat crackers and cheese.

C7
I like to eat crackers and cheese.

F
I like to eat crackers and cheese.

C7   F
Yum-yummy-yum-yum-yum!

Repeat, each time letting your children substitute names of different foods for crackers and cheese.

     Barbara Backer
     Charleston, SC

Now It's Time for Snack

Sung to: Here We Go Looby Loo

C
Now it is time for snack.

           G7
Now it is time for snack.

C
Now it is time for snack.

     G7   C
We will sit down and eat crackers.

Substitute the name of the day's snack for the word crackers.

     Susan Miller
     Kutztown, PA

Published by Totline Publications. Copyright protected.

1-57029-521-2 *Piggyback Songs—School Days*

Snack Time

Have You Ever Had an Apple?

Sung to: Have You Ever Seen a Lassie?

        C   G
Have you ever had an apple, an apple,
    C
an apple?

Have you ever had an apple

  G   C
And heard it go, "Crunch"?

            C   G
Have you ever had an orange, an orange,
    C
an orange?

Have you ever had an orange

  G   C
And heard it go, "Slurp"?

            C   G
Have you ever had a banana, a banana,
    C
a banana?

Have you ever had a banana

  G   C
And heard it go, "Mush"?

Frank Dally
Akeny, IA

My Sipping Straw

Sung to: The Muffin Man

G
Watch me use my sipping straw,

My sipping straw, my sipping straw.

G
Watch me use my sipping straw

  D7   G
To sip and sip and sip.

  G
I use my straw to sip my juice,

C
Sip my juice, sip my juice.

G
I use my staw to sip my juice.

  D7   G
I sip and sip and sip.

Repeat, substituting milk *for* juice.

Elizabeth McKinnon

Snacktime Rap

Sung to: Teddy Bear, Teddy Bear

F
Children, children, it's time to eat.

C7
Go wash your hands and have a seat.

F
Serve the food and eat it up.

                                     C   F
Talk with your friends and then clean up.

Nanette Belice and Kristina Carle
Kensington, MD

Snack Time

1-57029-521-2 *Piggyback Songs—School Days*

Lunch Is On the Way

Sung to: The Farmer in the Dell

F
The lunch is on the way; the lunch is on the
way.

                                          C7   F
Heigh-ho the derry-o, the lunch is on the way.

We all will eat our food; we all will eat our food.

                                   C7   F
Heigh-ho the derry-o, we all will eat our food.

The food will help us grow; the food will help
us grow.

                                   C7   F
Heigh-ho the derry-o, the food will help us grow.

And then we'll take our naps; and then we'll
take our naps.

                                     C7
Heigh-ho the derry-o, and then we'll take our
         F
naps.

And we will grow some more; and we will
grow some more.

                                C7
Heigh-ho the derry-o, YES we will grow
         F
some more!

Pauline Laughter
Tulsa, OK

Wash for Lunch

Sung to: London Bridge

C
We have washed our hands and faces,

G   C
Hands and faces, hands and faces.

We have washed our hands and faces.

G   C
May we eat lunch now?

Additional Verses: Germs are gone, they've
left no traces; We are sitting in our places.

Becky Valenick
Rockford, IL

Lunch with All the Bunch

Sung to: The Muffin Man

F
Now it's time to have some lunch,

G7   C7
Time to lunch with all the bunch.

F
Now it's time to have some lunch.

   G7   C7   F
Let's munch with all the bunch.

Betty Silkunas
Lansdale, PA

I'm Getting Very Hungry

Sung to: Frere Jacques

C
Time for lunch, time for lunch.

Let's get ready, let's get ready.

I'm getting very hungry.

I'm getting very hungry.

How 'bout you? How 'bout you?

C
Wash our hands, wash our hands

Before we eat, before we eat.

We should have clean hands.

We should have clean hands

When we eat, when we eat.

C
Let's sit down. Let's sit down

Quietly, quietly.

Wait 'til we are served.

Wait 'til we are served

Before we eat, before we eat.

C
Use table manners. Use table manners.

Let's be polite. Let's be polite.

Remember please and thank you.

Remember please and thank you

When we eat, when we eat.

Cindy Dingwall
Palatine, IL

Lunchtime

Sung to: Alouette

　　F
It's time for lunch now,

C7　　　　　　F
Yes, it's time for lunch now.

It's time for lunch now,

C7　　　　　F
Everyone line up.

Think of all the food we'll eat.

Think of all the food we'll eat.

C
Sandwiches, vegetables,

Milk and meat.

　　F
It's time for lunch now.

C7　　　　　　F
Yes, it's time for lunch now.

It's time for lunch now.

C7　　　　F
Everyone line up.

Judy Hall
Wytheville, VA

Lunch Time

It Is Naptime

Sung to: Frere Jacques

C
It is naptime, it is naptime.

Come along, come along.

Go and get your mat now.

Time to take a nap now.

Let's all rest. Let's all rest.

> Judy Hall
> Wytheville, VA

A Sleepy Bear

Sung to: Yankee Doodle

   C   G7
A sleepy bear crawls in its cave

    C   G7
And sleeps all winter long.

    C   F
But Jane will take just a little nap,

 G7   C
As soon as we finish this song.

Sing the song for each of your children,
substituting the child's name for Jane.

> Laura Egge
> Lake Oswego, OR

The Night-Night Song

Sung to: Brahms' Lullaby

                   C
Close your eyes. Close your eyes.

                        G7
Close your eyes and go nite-nite.

C
Close your eyes. Close your eyes.

Close your eyes and sleep so tight.

       F   C
Go to sleep little toes.

      G7   C
You've worked hard all day.

       F   C
Go to sleep little legs.

      G7   C
You've run hard and played.

(Repeat the first four lines.)

      F   C   G7   C
Go to sleep little hands. You're always so busy.

      F   C   G7   C
Go to sleep little arms. Being small isn't easy.

(Repeat the first four lines.)

      F   C   G7   C
Go to sleep little ears. There's so much to hear.

      F   C   G7   C
Go to sleep little mouth. There's nothing to fear.

(Repeat the first four lines.)

> Sharon Sweat
> West End, NC

Nap Time

Close Your Eyes

Sung to: Rock-A-Bye, Baby

C   G7
Now it is time for us to rest,

                    C
Close your eyes and do your best.

                 G7
I'll stay with you while you sleep.

C   F   G7   C
When you awake, we'll do something neat.

       Cindy Dingwall
       Palatine, IL

Time to Rest

Sung to: Oh, My Darling Clementine

C
Time to rest, time to rest—

                         G7
Sleepy heads, it's time to rest.

                          C
When you wake up, you'll feel so good,

             G7   C
That you'll do your very best!

       Janice Bodenstedt
       Jackson, MI

If You're Tired and You Know It

Sung to: If You're Happy and You Know It

        F   C
If you're tired and you know it, take a nap.

                        F
If you're tired and you know it, take a nap.

        B♭
If you're tired and you know it,

      F
Then your eyes will surely show it.

        C   F
If you're tired and you know it, take a nap.

       Stefanie Bair
       Kent, OH

Close Your Eyes

Sung to: Frere Jacques

C
Kyle is sleepy. Kyle is sleepy.

Close your eyes. Close your eyes.

It's time to go to sleep now.

Let's not hear a peep now.

Rest well, Kyle. Rest well, Kyle.

Sing the song for each of your children, substituting the child's name for Kyle.

       Laura Egge
       Lake Oswego, OR

 1-57029-521-2 *Piggyback Songs—School Days*

Ready for Bed

Sung to: Twinkle, Twinkle, Little Star

C   F   C
Here is Teddy, ready for bed.

G7 C   G7 C
Lay him down and rest his head.

C   G7 C G7
Cover him up so he won't peep.

C   G7 C G7
Watch him till he's fast a-sleep.

C   F   C
Here is Teddy, ready for bed.

G7 C   G7 C
Lay him down and rest his head.

Give your children a teddy bear or a similar toy to "sing to sleep" at nap time.

Adapted Traditional

Hush, Little Dolly

Sung to: Hush, Little Baby

F   C7
Hush, little dolly, don't you cry.

        F
I'm going to sing you a lullaby.

      C7
If you nap with me today,

         F
I'll wake you later so we can play.

Give each of your children a doll or a stuffed toy to sing to at nap time.

Laura Egge
Lake Oswego, OR

Wake Up, Sleepy Heads

Sung to: Yankee Doodle

C   G7
Hey, you sleepy heads, wake up!

     C   G
You cannot sleep all day.

     C   F
It's time to open up your eyes

G7   C
So we can run and play.

F
Find your shoes and put them on.

    C
We'll put your cot away.

F
We are rested from our naps

    C   G7   C
And now we want to play.

Frank Dally
Ankeny, IA

1-57029-521-2 *Piggyback Songs—School Days*

Nap Time

Stretch, Stretch, Stretch Your Arms

Sung to: Row, Row, Row Your Boat

C
Stretch, stretch, stretch your arms

High above your head.

Stretch so high.

Reach the sky.

And then we'll stretch again.
(Children stretch high as they can while singing.)

Saundra Winnett
Fort Worth, TX

Stretching, Stretching, Boys and Girls

Sung to: Twinkle, Twinkle, Little Star

C   F   C
Stretching, stretching, tall and far—

G7   C   G7   C
Show the world who you are.

C   G7   C   G7
Stretching, stretching to the sky

C   G7 C   G7
Boys and girls, reach up high.

C   F   C
Stretching, stretching, tall and far—

G7   C   G7   C
Reach a-bove the moon and stars.

Saundra Winnett
Fort Worth, TX

Reach Up and Touch the Sky

Sung to: If You're Happy and You Know It

F   C
Oh, I wish I could reach up and touch the sky.
(Stretch arms high.)

                              F
Oh, I wish I could reach up and touch the sky.

       B♭
Oh, if I could touch the sky,

      F
Then I'd get up there and fly.
(Wave arms up and down.)

  C   F
Oh, I wish I could reach up and touch the sky.

Laura Egge
Lake Oswego, OR

Movement Time—Stretching

58

1-57029-521-2 Piggyback Songs—School Days

I Can Bend and Touch the Floor

Sung to: Mary Had a Little Lamb

F
I can bend and touch the floor,

C   F
Touch the floor, touch the floor.

F
Put your hands on the floor;

C   F
Now let's walk a-round.

     Saundra Winnett
     Fort Worth, TX

Stand Up Name Song

Sung to: Frere Jacques

F
Stand up, Ruthie. Stand up, Ruthie.

Stand up, John. Stand up, John.

Reach up very high, now.

Reach up to the sky, now.

Then sit down. Then sit down.

     Kathleen Sparks
     Syracuse, NY

Everyone Hold Hands

Sung to: The Farmer in the Dell

D
Everyone hold hands.

Let's go and turn around.

Shake your shoulders back and forth,

   A7   D
Then bend and touch the ground.

D
Reach up and touch the sky.

Stretch up very high.

Touch your toes, then touch your nose.

A7   D
Reach up and touch the sky.

     Juanita Veeley
     Louisville, KY

Movement Time—Stretching

Hands That Clap

Sung to: Mary Had a Little Lamb

F
(Child's name) has two hands that clap,

C   F
Hands that clap, hands that clap.

F
(Child's name) has two hands that clap.

C   F
Clap and turn a-round.

Procedure: Form a circle. One child is in center of circle, acting out movement. All sing.

Additional Verses: Feet that jump; Feet that dance; Arms that stretch; Hands that shake, etc.

Saundra Winnett
Fort Worth, TX

Moving Song

Sung to: Jingle Bells

F
Clap your hands. Stomp your feet.
  Wiggle all around.

C7   F
Reach your hands high in the air,

  G7   C7
And now let's touch the ground.

F
Hold your head. Hold your hips.
  Give yourself a hug.

C7   F
Lie down flat up-on the ground,

  C7   F
But watch out for the bugs.

Diana Nazaruk
Clark Lake, MI

Clap Your Hands

Sung to: Row, Row, Row Your Boat

C
Clap, clap, clap your hands
(Clap and sing slowly.)

As slowly as can be.

Clap them, clap them,

Clap them, clap them.

Do it now with me.

C
Clap, clap, clap your hands
(Clap and sing fast.)

As fast as fast can be.

Clap them, clap them,

Clap them, clap them.

Do it now with me.

Additional Verses: Roll, roll, roll your hands; Wave, wave, wave your hands; Stomp, stomp, stomp your feet; Tap, tap, tap your toes.

Adapted Traditional

Movement Time—Clapping

1-57029-521-2 *Piggyback Songs—School Days*

Here's a Game

Sung to: Bingo

F   Bb F
Here's a game that's lots of fun,

       C F
And this is how we play it.

    Bb
Hop, hop, hop, hop, hop.
(Hop.)

C   F
Skip, skip, skip, skip, skip.
(Skip.)

Bb
Turn, turn, turn, turn, turn.
(Turn in a circle.)

      C   F
And that is how we play it.

Continue with similar verses, substituting other movements for those in the song.

Laura Egge
Lake Oswego, OR

Stretch, Jump, and Bend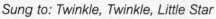

Sung to: Twinkle, Twinkle, Little Star

C   F C
Stretching, stretching, way up high;
(Stretch.)

G7 C G7 C
Stretching, stretching to the sky.

C   G7 C   G7
Stretching out and stretching in;

C   G7 C G7
Stretching is how we be-gin.

C   F C
Stretching, stretching, way up high.

G7 C G7 C
Stretching, stretching to the sky.

C   F C
Jumping, jumping, all a-round;
(Jump.)

G7 C G7 C
Jumping, jumping on the ground.

C   G7 C G7
Jumping fast and jumping slow;

C G7 C G7
Jumping is the way to go.

C   F C
Jumping, jumping all a-round.

G7 C G7 C
Jumping, jumping on the ground.

C   F   C
Bending, bending, bend our knees;
(Bend.)

G7 C G7   C
Bending, bending—watch us, please.

C G7 C   G7
Bending, bending way down low;

C   G7 C   G7
Bending's lots of fun, you know.

C   F   C
Bending, bending, bend our knees.

G7 C G7 C
Bending, bending—watch us please.

Barbara B. Fleisher
Glen Oaks, NY

Let's Pretend

Sung to: Three Blind Mice

C   G7 C   G7 C
Let's pre-tend. Let's pre-tend.

  G7   C   G7   C
What can I do? What can I do?

   G7   C
I can crawl like a little crab.
(Crawl around sideways.)

   G7   C
I can crawl like a little crab.

   G7   C
I can crawl like a little crab.

   G7   C
Crawl, crawl, crawl.

C   G7 C   G7 C
Let's pre-tend. Let's pre-tend.

  G7   C   G7   C
What can I do? What can I do?

   G7   C
I can hop like a kangaroo.
(Hop around.)

   G7   C
I can hop like a kangaroo.

   G7   C
I can hop like a kangaroo.

   G7 C
Hop, hop, hop.

Continue with similar verses, such as I can
wiggle just like a worm, *or* I can jump like a
little frog.

Laura Egge
Lake Oswego, OR

Toes Are Tapping

Sung to: Skip to My Lou

C
Hands are clapping, clap, clap, clap.

G7
Hands are clapping, clap, clap, clap.

C
Hands are clapping, clap, clap, clap.

G7   C
Clap your hands, my darling.

C
Toes are tapping, tap, tap, tap.

G7
Toes are tapping, tap, tap, tap.

C
Toes are tapping, tap, tap, tap.

G7   C
Tap your toes, my darling.

Also use: Arms are swinging; Fingers are
wiggling; Eyes are blinking; Tongues are
clicking; Heads are nodding; Fists are
pounding; Hips are twisting; Elbows are
bending, etc.

Barbara Jackson
Denton, TX

Movement Time

Hands Up High ✓

Sung to: London Bridge

C
First we wave our hands up high,

G
Hands up high, hands up high.

C
First we wave our hands up high,

G   C
Then we clap them.

C
Then we shake our hands down low,

G
Hands down low, hands down low.

C
Then we shake our hands down low,

G   C
Then we hide them.

Continue with other body parts, such as: move
our feet so quiet, then we stop them; *or* move
our arms to the side, then we cross them;
move our heads all around, then we rest them;
stand up straight and tall, then we sit down.

Barb Robinson
Huntington Beach, CA

The Shape-Up Song

Sung to: The Farmer in the Dell

C
We're jumping up and down.

We're jumping up and down.

We're getting lots of exercise.

G   C
We're jumping up and down.

2nd verse . . . We bend and touch our toes . . .

3rd verse . . . We kick our legs up high . . .

4th verse . . . We jog around the room . . .

5th verse . . . We wiggle our whole bodies . . .

6th verse . . . We stretch up to the sky . . .

Suzanne L. Harrington & Wendy Spaide
North Wales, PA

Moving Song

Sung to: Johnny Pounds with One Hammer

C
(Child's name) can walk to the table,

G   C
The table, the table.

C
(Child's name) can walk to the table,

G   C
Walk there now.

Additional Verses: (Paul) can march to the
wall; hop to the shelf; skip to the fence; *etc.*

Sister Linda Kaman R.S.M.
Pittsburg, PA

Movement Time

1-57029-521-2 *Piggyback Songs—School Days*

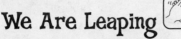

We Are Leaping

Sung to: Frere Jacques

C
We are leaping. We are leaping.

Leap, leap, leap; leap, leap, leap.

Now let's all start twirling.

Now let's all start twirling.

Twirl, twirl, twirl; twirl, twirl, twirl.

C
We are crawling. We are crawling.

Crawl, crawl, crawl; crawl, crawl, crawl.

Now let's all start rolling.

Now let's all start rolling.

Roll, roll, roll; roll, roll, roll.

Continue with similar verses, substituting other movements for those in the song.

> Laura Egge
> Lake Oswego, OR

March Along

Sung to: This Old Man

C
March along! March along!

F   G
Life your feet up off the ground!

      C
And we'll march and sing a happy little song,

G   C   G7 C
As we go march-ing on!

> Diana Nazuruk
> Clark Lake, MI

I Am Turning

Sung to: Frere Jacques

F
I am turning. I am turning,

'Round and 'round; 'round and 'round.

First I go one way.

Then I go the other way.

Touch the ground. Now sit down.

Additional Verses: I am dancing; I am marching; I am chugging; I am flying; I am moving; I am spinning.

> Susan Widdifield
> Poulsbo, WA

Monkey See and Do

Sung to: Twinkle, Twinkle, Little Star

C   F   C
Monkey see, and monkey do.

G7 C   G7   C
Monkey does the same as you.

C   G7   C   G7
We are watching what you do.

C   G7   C   G7
And we do the same thing, too.

C   F   C
Monkey see, and monkey do.

G7 C   G7   C
Monkey does the same as you.

Each time you sing the song, let one of your children make movements and have the others imitate him or her.

> Laura Egge
> Lake Oswego, OR

Movement Time

1-57029-521-2 *Piggyback Songs—School Days*

It's Time to Go Outside

Sung to: The Farmer in the Dell

D
It's time to go outside.

It's time to go outside.

Let's walk to the door.

A7   D
It's time to go out-side.

Substitute a different action word, such as
skip, crawl, *or* tiptoe, *for* walk.

    Nadine Haskell
    Kent, OH

Time to Go Out and Play

Sung to: The Bear Went Over the Mountain

D   G D
It's time to go out and play.

 A7   D
It's time to go out and play.

            G
It's time to go out and play

  A7   D
With all our friends to-day.

    Judy Hall
    Wytheville, VA

Outside Play

Sung to: Twinkle, Twinkle, Little Star

C   F   C
Let's go out to play to-day.

    G7   C   G7   C
The sun is shining; it's a beautiful day.

    G7   C   G7
We will hop and skip and run,

C   G7   C G7
And we'll have a lot of fun.

C   F   C
Let's go out to play to-day.

    G7   C   G7   C
The sun is shining; it's a beautiful day.

    Patricia Coyne
    Mansfield, MA

Now It's Time to Play Outside

Sung to: Ten Little Indians

C
Now it's time to play outside;

G7
Now it's time to play outside;

C
Now it's time to play outside

G7   C
Where it's sunny and warm.

Additional Verses: Now it's time to run and
play; Now it's time to throw the ball; Now it's
time to jump rope; etc.

    Sue St. John
    Oregon, OH

To the Playground Today

Sung to: The Mulberry Bush

D
We're going to the playground today,

A7
Playground today, playground today.

D
We're going to the playground today,

  A7   D
To play out in the sun.

D
Perhaps we'll play on the swings today,

A7
Swings today, swings today.

D
Perhaps we'll play on the swings today.

  A7   D
Let's go and have some fun.

Continue with similar verses, each time substituting the name of a different piece of playground equipment for swings.

Kathy McCullough
St. Charles, IL

Down by the Playground

Sung to: Down by the Station

C   G   C
Down by the playground, early in the morning,

                    G   C
See the little seesaws all in a row.

All the swings and monkey bars,

G   C
And the slides are waiting—

              G
Waiting for the children:

        C
Ready, set, go!

Judy Hall
Wytheville, VA

Playing All Morning

Sung to: I've Been Working on the Railroad

G
We've been playing on the playground

C   G
All the morning long.

We've been playing on the playground.

    D7   G
Having fun and singing songs.

Barbara Robinson
Glendale, AR

1-57029-521-2 *Piggyback Songs—School Days*

Out on the Playground

Sung to: Up on the Housetop

D
Playing on the playground is a treat.

G   D   A
Swinging and sliding can't be beat.

     D
The playground is where we like to play.

G D   A   D
It is fun each and every day.

G   D
Fun, fun, fun, we like to run.

A   D
Fun, fun, fun, 'til we are done.

              G
The playground is where we like to play.

D   A   D
It is fun each and every day.

    Judy Hall
    Wytheville, VA

Climbing up the Slide

Sung to: The Eensy, Weensy Spider

    F   C7   F
My itsy bitsy feet are climbing up the slide.

                C7   F
Down comes my body in a long glide.

                C7   F
Up go my feet again, inching to the top.

                C7   F
Down I slide so quickly to a great, big stop.

    Judy Hall
    Wytheville, VA

Playground Fun

Sung to: Take Me Out to the Ball Game

C   G
Let's go out to the playground,

C   G
Let's go out to the swings.

A7   Dm
Seesaws and sliding boards, climbers, too;

                         G
I like the jungle gym. How about you?

             C   G
For it's run, jump, slide at the playground.

           C   F
If you don't have fun, it's a shame.

           F   C
Oh, let's sing, play, have a good day

           F   G   C
At the play-ground to-day.

    Betty Silkunas
    Lansdale, PA

Exercise Our Muscles

Sung to: Ring Around the Rosie

C
Run around the playground.

Exercise our muscles—

                  G   C
Growing, growing up so strong.

Additional Verses: Swing on the swings; Climb
on the bars; Dig in the sandbox; Bounce,
bounce the balls.

    Susan Peters
    Upland, CA

Outdoor Time—Playground

Sliding

Sung to: Row, Row, Row Your Boat

C
Climb, climb up the slide,
(Sing slowly.)

Climb up to the top.

Sliding, sliding down the slide,
(Sing fast.)

Slide until you stop.

> Elizabeth McKinnon

Let's Go to the Playground

Sung to: Did You Ever See a Lassie?

F
Let's go to the playground,

   C7   F
The playground, the playground.

Let's go to the playground

C7   F
Where we will swing.

   C7   F
We'll swing and swing,

    C7   F
And swing and swing.

Let's go to the playground

C7   F
Where we will swing.

Substitute the names of other playground activities for the word swing.

> Susan Miller
> Kutztown, PA

Playground Song

Sung to: Mary Had a Little Lamb

C
I like to climb on the jungle gym,

G7   C
Jungle gym, jungle gym.

I like to climb on the jungle gym

G7   C
On the big play-ground.

  C
I like to go up in the swing,

G7   C
In the swing, in the swing.

I like to go up in the swing

G7   C
On the big play-ground.

  C
I like to go down the steep slide,

G7   C
The steep slide, the steep slide.

I like to go down the steep slide

G7   C
On the big play-ground.

> Barbara B. Fleisher
> Glen Oaks, NY

Outdoor Time—Playground

The Swinging Song

Sung to: Twinkle, Twinkle, Little Star

C   F   C
Swing on your tummy; swing on your seat.

G7   C   G7   C
Pump with your hands and knees and feet.

C   G7   C   G7
Point your toes up in the air.

C   G7   C   G7
Feel the wind blow through your hair.

C   F   C
When you're high up in a swing,

G7   C   G7 C
You can do most any-thing!

Diane Thom
Maple Valley, WA

Swinging, Swinging

Sung to: Sailing, Sailing

C   F   C
Swinging, swinging, on my special swing;

   G7   C
When days are hot and days are cold,

D   G7
Swinging on my swing.

C   F   C
Up high, down low, now reach for the sky.

  G7   C
Oh, don't you wish that you were me,

D   G C
Swinging up so high?

Susan Nydick
Philadelphia, PA

I Am Swinging

Sung to: Frere Jacques

C
I am swinging. I am swinging

Up so high, up so high.

First I swing forward,

Then I swing backward.

Touch the sky. Touch the sky.

Susan Nydick
Philadelphia, PA

1-57029-521-2 *Piggyback Songs—School Days*

Outdoor Time—Swinging

Riding on My Scooter

Sung to: The Little White Duck

   F
I'm riding on my scooter.

         C
Watch me going past.

I'm riding on my scooter,

      F
Going very fast.

         C
I like to ride around, you see.

        F
Riding's so much fun for me.

Oh, I'm riding on my scooter.

         C
Watch me going past.

      F
Going very fast!

*Repeat, each time substituting the name of a
different riding toy for scooter.*

Gayle Bittinger

I Love Sand

Sung to: Three Blind Mice

C   G7   C   G7 C
Sand, sand, sand; sand, sand, sand.

 G7 C   G7 C
I love sand. I love sand.

        G7   C
It's fun to squish it be-tween my toes,

        G7   C
Or build a mountain as high as my nose,

        G7   C
Or dig a tunnel that grows and grows,

        G7 C
'Cause I love sand.

Susan Hodges

Outdoor Time

1-57029-521-2 *Piggyback Songs—School Days*

Time to Clean Up

Sung to: Oh, My Darling Clementine

> F
> Time to clean up; time to clean up;

> C7
> Time to clean up right a-way.

> F
> Time to clean up; time to clean up,

> C7   F
> 'Cause now it's time to play.

Additional Verses: Stack your crayons, Pick up your trash; Fix your papers; Pack up your things.

> Lois Putnam
> Pilot Mt., NC

It's Time to Stop Now

Sung to: London Bridge

> C
> It's time to stop now and clean up,

> G   C
> And clean up, and clean up.

> It's time to stop now and clean up,

> G   C
> Then we'll have our snack.

Substitute the name of the next activity for the phrase have our snack.

> Ann-Marie Donovan
> Framingham, MA

Let's Clean Up

Sung to: Frere Jacques

> C
> Playtime's over; playtime's over.

> Let's clean up; let's clean up.

> Then we'll join the circle.

> Then we'll join the circle

> For more fun, for more fun.

> Melissa Leonard
> Minersville, PA

1-57029-521-2 *Piggyback Songs—School Days*

Clean-Up Time

Sung to: Happy Birthday to You

    F   C
It's time to clean (pick) up.

            F
It's time to clean up.

           B♭
It's time to clean u-up.

     F   C F
Put the toys on the shelf.
(in the box, in the drawer, etc.)

   F   C
I need you to help.
(can substitute the name of a child.)

         F
I need you to help.

         B♭
I need you to help me.

   F   C F
Put this book on the shelf.
(truck on the floor, etc.)

   F   C
I like what I see.

        F
I like what I see.

        B♭
I like what I see-ee.

   F   C F
You clean up so well!

    Renee Lowry
    Canoga Park, CA

It's Time to Clean Up

Sung to: Mary Had a Little Lamb

C
Do you know what time it is,

G7   C
Time it is, time it is?

Do you know what time it is?

  G7   C
It's time to clean up.

    Betty Ruth Baker
    Waco, TX

We Are Cleaning

Sung to: If You're Happy and You Know It

        F   C
We are cleaning all the tables. Watch us now.

                             F
We are cleaning all the tables. We know how.

    B♭
We are scrubbing high and low.

    F
We are scrubbing fast and slow.

    C   F
We are cleaning all the tables. Watch us now.

Repeat, each time substituting the name of the item your children are cleaning for tables.

    Gayle Bittinger

1-57029-521-2 *Piggyback Songs—School Days*

Cleanup Time—Clean Up

Pick Up the Blocks

Sung to: The Paw Paw Patch

F
Pick up the blocks and put them on the shelf.

C
Pick up the blocks and put them on the shelf.

F
Pick up the blocks and put them on the shelf.

    C   F
Un-til our room is clean.

F
Thank you, Johnny; you're a big help.

C
Thank you, Johnny; you're a big help.

F
Thank you, Johnny; you're a big help.

C   F
Now our room is all cleaned up.

    Jean Warren

We're Picking Up Our Toys

Sung to: The Farmer in the Dell

      D
We're picking up our toys.

We're picking up our toys.

Heigh-ho-the-derry-oh!

           A7   D
We're picking up our toys.

Additional Verses: We're picking up our books; We're picking up our puzzles; We're picking up our games; *etc.*

    Lois Olson
    Webster City, IA

Time to Pick Up the Toys

Sung to: Mary Had a Little Lamb

    C
It's time to pick the toys up now,

G   C
Toys up now, toys up now.

Time to pick the toys up now.

    G   C
Let's see who does the best.

    Diana Nazaruk
    Clark, Lake, MI

1-57029-521-2 *Piggyback Songs—School Days*

Let's Put Our Toys Away

Sung to: The Muffin Man

G
Let's put all our toys away,

    C   D7
Our toys away, our toys away.

G
Let's put all our toys away

    D7   G
Each in a special place!

> Maria Courtright
> Munroe Falls, OH

Time to Put Our Toys Away

Sung to: The Mulberry Bush

    D
It's time to put our toys away,

A
Toys away, toys away.

    D
It's time to put our toys away

A   D
So we can eat our lunch.

You may substitute other phrases for eat our
lunch *such as* play outside, go to music, *etc.*

> MaryAnn Adams
> Manassas, VA

After We Play

Sung to: Twinkle, Twinkle, Little Star

C   F   C
After we play with the toys,

    G7   C   G7   C
We join the other girls and boys

         G7   C   G7
In helping put the things a-way

    C   G7   C   G7
So we can play an-other day.

C   F   C
We're proud of the job we've done

  G7   C   G7   C
Be-cause it's shared by every-one.

> Susan Burbridge
> Beavercreek, OH

Cleanup Pokey

Sung to: Hokey Pokey

C
You pick your first block up.

You put your first block down.

You pick your next block up,

        G
And you shake it all around.

You do the cleanup pokey,

And you put your things away—

           C
That's what it's all a-bout.

> Judy Hall
> Wytheville, WA

Cleanup Time—Put Away

1-57029-521-2 *Piggyback Songs—School Days*

It's Time to Put Our Things Away

Sung to: Twinkle, Twinkle, Little Star

C   F   C
We've had lots of fun to-day.

   G7   C   G7   C
It's time to put our things a-way.

      G7   C   G7
We need all the girls and boys

   C   G7   C   G7
To stop right now and pick up toys.

C   F   C
We've had lots of fun to-day.

   G7   C   G7   C
It's time to put our things a-way.

Ann-Marie Donovan
Framingham, MA

Pick Up the Toys

Sung to: Ten Little Indians

C
Pick up the toys and put them away,

G7
Pick up the toys and put them away.

C
Pick up the toys and put them away.

G7   C
It is cleanup time.

Additional Verses: Pick up the puzzles and put them together; Pick up the books and put them on the shelf; Pick up the blocks and put them in the box; Look at the room, it's neat and tidy; Thank you, thank you all for helping.

Cindy Dingwall
Palatine, IL

Put Them All Away

Sung to: Skip to My Lou

F
Pick your toys up off the floor;

C7
Pick your toys up off the floor;

F
Pick your toys up off the floor

    C7   F
And put them all a-way.

Additional Verses: Pick your games up off the table; Pick your books up off the floor; etc.

Rita Galloway
Harlingen, TX

Let's Pick Up Today

Sung to: The Mulberry Bush

C
Let's pick up the blocks today,

   G
The blocks today, the blocks today.

C
Let's pick up the blocks today,

   G   C
And put them all a-way.

Additional Verses: Let's pick up the toys today; Let's pick up the books today; Let's pick up the puzzles today; etc.

Susan Miller
Kutztown, PA

Published by Totline Publications. Copyright protected.

1-57029-521-2 *Piggyback Songs—School Days*

Cleanup Time—Pick Up & Put Away

Pick Up Toys

Sung to: Frere Jacques

C
Girls and boys, girls and boys,

Pick up toys, pick up toys.

It's time to put the toys away.

Let's make it very clean today.

Thank you all. Thank you all.

> Laura Egge
> Lake Oswego, OR

Put Our Toys Away

Sung to: Mary Had a Little Lamb

C
Let's all put our toys away,

G7   C
Toys away, toys away.

Let's all put our toys away,

  G7   C
And sit down with our friends.

> Bev Qualheim
> Marquette, MI

This Is the Way

Sung to: The Mulberry Bush

D
This is the way we pick up toys,

A7
Pick up toys, pick up toys.

D
This is the way we pick up toys.

  A7   D
Our playtime now is over.

D
Rosie is picking up the blocks,

A7
Up the blocks, up the blocks.

D
Rosie is picking up the blocks.

  A7   D
Our playtime now is over.

D
Jason is putting the puzzles away,

A7
Puzzles away, puzzles away.

D
Jason is putting the puzzles away.

  A7   D
Our playtime now is over.

Sing a verse for each of your children,
substituting the child's name and his or her
cleanup activity for those in the song.

> Laura Egge
> Lake Oswego, OR

Cleanup Time—Pick Up & Put Away

Cleanup Time

Sung to: Happy Birthday

     F   C   F
It's time to clean up. It's time to clean up.

                  B♭   F   C F
It's time to clean up. Put the toys a-way.

     F   C   F
I need Sean to help. I need Sean to help.

                  B♭   F   C F
I need Sean to help me put this book a-way.

     F   C   F
I like what I see. I like what I see.

                  B♭   F   C F
I like what I see. You clean up so well.

*Substitute the name of one of your children
for the name* Sean, *and the name of an item
to be put away for the word* book.

Renee Lowry
Canoga Park, CA

Let's All Join In

Sung to: If You're Happy and You Know It

     G   D
It's cleanup time, let's all join in.

                                   G
It's cleanup time, let's all join in.

            C
All the girls and all the boys,

           G
Let's put away the toys.

     D   G
It's cleanup time, let's all join in.

Kristina Carle and Nanette Belice
Kensington, MD

Everyone's a Helper

Sung to: Frere Jacques

C
Time for cleanup; time for cleanup,

Everyone, everyone.

We all work together.

We all work together.

Cleanup time. Cleanup time.

C
Pick up the toys. Pick up the toys.

Put them away. Put them away.

Everyone's a helper.

Everyone's a helper.

Thank you, Zak. Thank you, Anne.

*Substitute the names of your children for the
names* Zak *and* Anne.

Linda Meisch
Lincoln Park, NJ

1-57029-521-2 *Piggyback Songs—School Days*

Cleanup Time

Playtime's Over

Sung to: London Bridge

C
Now it's time to pick up toys,

G7
Pick up toys, pick up toys.

Now it's time to pick up toys.

G7   C
Playtime's over.

C
Loni and Scott are cleaning up,

G7
Cleaning up, cleaning up.

Loni and Scott are cleaning up.

G7   C
Playtime's over.

*Repeat, each time substituting the names of
your children for those in the song.*

> Laura Egge
> Lake Oswego, OR

Cleanup Time Today

Sung to: Row, Row, Row Your Boat

C
Clean, clean, it's time to clean—

Cleanup time today.

Books and blocks and all your toys:

Put them all away.

> Carol Kyger
> Hood River, OR

Room Cleanup

Sung to: The Farmer in the Dell

D
We're cleaning up our room.

The job will be done soon.

It's fun to put the toys away

A7   D
While we sing a happy tune.

> Susan Burbridge
> Beavercreek, OH

Let's All Work Together

Sung to: Jingle Bells

F
Cleanup time, cleanup time,

Let's put the toys away.

C7   F
Let's all work to-gether now

G7   C
To clean our room to-day.

F
Cleanup time, cleanup time,

Let's put the toys away.

C7   F
Let's all work to-gether now

C7   F
To clean our room to-day.

> Rita Galloway
> Harlingen, TX

Cleanup Time

Put Your Work Away

Sung to: Twinkle, Twinkle, Little Star

C   F   C
Stop and put your work a-way;

G7 C   G7   C
It is time to end the day.

      G7   C   G7
We have worked, and we have played.

     C   G7   C   G7
We'll come a-gain an-other day.

C   F   C
Stop and put your work a-way.

G7 C   G7   C
It is time to end the day.

> Betty Ruth Baker
> Waco, TX

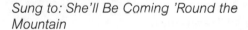

We'll Be Ready for Our Parents

Sung to: She'll Be Coming 'Round the Mountain

      F
We'll be ready for our parents when they come.

                       C7
We'll be ready for our parents when they come.

      F
We'll be sitting nice and quiet;

       B♭
Please get ready, won't you try it?

      F   C7   F
We'll be ready for our parents when they come.

> Cindy Dingwall
> Palatine, IL

Our Day Is Done

Sung to: The Farmer in the Dell

D
Now our day is done.

We've all had lots of fun.

Tomorrow is another day.

              A7   D
And we'll come back to play.

> Kerry L. Stanley
> Centre Square, PA

Our Friends

Sung to: Mary Had a Little Lamb

C
Taylor played on the slide today,

G7   C
Slide today, slide today.

Taylor played on the slide today.

G7   C
Taylor is our friend.

C
Gina was a helper today,

G7   C
Helper today, helper today.

Gina was a helper today.

G7   C
Gina is our friend.

Sing similar verses for your children, substituting their names for those in the song.

> Laura Egge
> Lake Oswego, OR

79

Daily Good-bye Song

Sung to: Yankee Doodle

C   G7
Now it's time to say good-bye;

      C   G7
We've had a lot of fun.

C   F
Good-bye, good-bye, good-bye, good-bye,

     G7   C
Our time at school is done.

F
Now it's time to say good-bye;

      C
We've had a lot of fun.

F
Good-bye, good-bye, good-bye, good-bye,

     C   G7   C
Our time at school is done.

Linda Ferguson
Olympia, WA

Good-bye Song

Sung to: Goodnight, Ladies

F   C
Good-bye Brian, good-bye Cindy,

F   B♭   F   C   F
Good-bye Andy; it's time to say good-bye.

Substitute the names of your children for the names in the song. Shake hands with each child as his or her name is sung. Repeat until each child's name has been sung.

Paula Laughtland
Edmonds, WA

Good-bye

Sung to: My Darling Clementine

     C
Adi-ós, adiós,

                     G
Adiós means good-bye.

     F   C
Adi-ós, adi-ós,

     G   C
We'll see you next time!

Sue Thomas

Spanish Pronunciation

Ah-dee-OHS, ah-dee-OHS,
Ah-dee-OHS means good-bye.
Ah-dee-OHS, ah-dee-OHS,
We'll see you next time!

English Translation

Good-bye, good-bye,
Good-bye means good-bye.
Good-bye, good-bye,
We'll see you next time!

Wave Good-bye

Sung to: Row, Row, Row Your Boat

C
Wave, wave, wave your hands;

Wave them low and high.

Wave them, wave them, wave them, wave them

When you say good-bye.

Shana Sloan

Learning & Caring

I'm Getting Better Every Day

Sung to: Row, Row, Row Your Boat

C
I'm learning how to count,

I'm learning how to count.

I'm getting better every day.

I'm learning how to count.

Additional Verses: I'm learning how to write; I'm learning how to draw; I'm learning all the letters; I'm learning how to read; etc.

Ann-Marie Donovan
Framingham, MA

If You Get Lost

Sung to: Yankee Doodle

F   C
If you get lost on any street,

F   C
Don't talk to a stranger.

      F
Look for a policeman and he will

C   F
Keep you out of danger.

B♭
Tell him what your name is,

F
Where your house is, too.

B♭
He will help you get back home,

    C   F
Or bring your mom to you!

Judy Hall
Wytheville, VA

Dial 9-1-1

Sung to: London Bridge

    C
Dial 9-1-1 when you need help,

G7   C
You need help, you need help.

Dial 9-1-1 when you need help.

G7   C
They will help you.

Laura Egge
Lake Oswego, OR

What Would You Do?

Sung to: London Bridge

C
What would you do if your house caught fire,

G7   C
House caught fire, house caught fire?

What would you do if your house caught fire?

G7   C
What would you do?
(Encourage children to respond.)

Substitute similar phrases about other safety-related situations, such as if your mom fell down *or* if a stranger offered a ride, *for* if your house caught fire.

Laura Egge
Lake Oswego, OR

Who Are You?

Sung to: Frere Jacques

C
What's your name? What's your name?
(Adult sings.)

Adam Smith. Adam Smith.
(Child responds.)

What is your street?
(Adult sings.)

What is your street?

Summit Drive. Summit Drive.
(Child responds.)

Sing the song for each of your children.

Laura Egge
Lake Oswego, OR

It's Important That I Know My Address

Sung to: If You're Happy and You Know It

      F   C7
It's im-portant that I know my ad-dress.

                             F
It's important that I know my ad-dress.

       Bb
If you listen to me now,

      F
I will say it. I know how.

      C7   F
It's im-portant that I know my ad-dress.

Have each child say his or her address at the end of the song.

Cindy Dingwall
Palatine, IL

Seven Little Numbers

Sung to: I'm a Little Teapot

C   F   C
Seven little numbers on my phone,

 G7   C   G7   C
I learn them to-gether to call my home.

                  F   C
Seven little numbers, what are they?

F   C   G7   C
My phone number I learned to-day.

Have each child say his or her phone number at the end of the song.

Carla Cotter Skjong
Tyler, MN

My Phone Number

Sung to: The Muffin Man

Adult sings:

      G
Oh, do you know your phone number

      C   D7
Your phone number, your phone number?

      G
Oh, do you know your phone number?

 D7   G
5-5-5-1-2-3-4.

Child responds:

      G
Oh, yes, I know my phone number,

      C   D7
My phone number, my phone number.

      G
Oh, yes, I know my phone number.

 D7   G
5-5-5-1-2-3-4.

Sing the song for each of your children, substituting the child's phone number for the one in the song.

Laura Egge
Lake Oswego, OR

1-57029-521-2 *Piggyback Songs—School Days*

Safety—Information

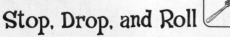

Stop, Drop, and Roll

Sung to: Oh, My Darling Clementine

F
If my clothes catch on fire,

                   C
I will know just what to do.

              F
I will stop all of my running.

         C7   F
Drop and roll's the thing to do.

      Becky Valenick
      Rockford, IL

Never Play with Matches

Sung to: Frere Jacques

F
Never, never play with matches.

If you do, if you do,

You might burn your fingers.

You might burn your fingers.

That won't do. That won't do.

Other possible ending:

You might start a fire.

You might start a fire.

That won't do. That won't do.

      Leora Grecian
      San Bernardino, CA

Stop, Drop, and Roll

Sung to: Skip to My Lou

F
Stop, stop, stop, drop and roll.

C7
Stop, stop, stop, drop and roll.

F
Stop, stop, stop, drop and roll

C7   F
If your clothes catch on fire.

F
Don't run, whatever you do.

C7
Don't run, whatever you do.

F
Don't run, whatever you do.

C7   F
Just roll to put out the fire.

Let your children practice rolling on the floor as you sing the song.

      Laura Egge
      Lake Oswego, OR

Safety—Fire

We Stop, Look, and Listen

Sung to: Row, Row, Row Your Boat

C
We stop, look, and listen

Before we cross the street.

First we use our eyes and ears.

Then we use our feet.

     Adapted Traditional

Stop, Look, and Listen

Sung to: Skip to My Lou

C
Stop, look; stop, look and listen;

G7
Stop, look; stop, look and listen;

C
Stop, look; stop, look and listen,

  G7   C
Be-fore you cross the street.

     Lois Putnam
     Pilot Mt., NC

When I Cross the Street

Sung to: Have You Ever Seen a Lassie?

      C
Wh-en I cross the street,

    G   C
The street, the street;

      C
Wh-en I cross the street,

    G   C
I make sure that I'm safe.

    G   C
I look this way and that way,

    G   C
And that way and this way.

      C
Wh-en I cross the street,

    G   C
I make sure that I'm safe.

     Frank Dally
     Akeny, IA

Safety—Crossing Streets

1-57029-521-2 *Piggyback Songs—School Days*

When We Go to School

Sung to: Mary Had a Little Lamb

C
This is the way we watch the lights,

G7   C
Watch the lights, watch the lights.

This is the way we watch the lights,

G7   C
When we go to school.

   C
We stop and wait if it is red,

 G7   C
If it is red, if it is red.

We stop and wait if it is red,

G7   C
When we go to school.

Additional Verses:
We wait until the light turns green.
We look both ways before we cross.
We walk directly to our school.

Sue St. John
Oregon, OH

Twinkle, Twinkle Traffic Light

Sung to: Twinkle, Twinkle Little Star

C   F   C
Twinkle, twinkle traffic light

G7   C   G7   C
Shining on the corner bright.

C   G7   C   G7
When it's green it's time to go,

C   G7   C   G7
When it's red, it's stop, you know.

C   F   C
Twinkle, twinkle traffic light

G7   C   G7   C
Shining on the corner bright.

Mrs. Gary McNitt
Adrian, MI

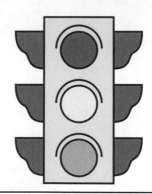

Colors of Safety

Sung to: Twinkle, Twinkle, Little Star

C   F   C
Red means stop, and green means go;

G7   C   G7   C
Yellow's caution, we all know.

       G7   C   G7
Stoplights tell cars what to do.

C   G7   C   G7
We'll pre-tend that we're cars, too.

C   F   C
Red means stop, and green means go;

G7   C   G7   C
Yellow's caution, we all know.

Becky Valenick
Rockford, IL

Buckle Up

Sung to: A-Hunting We Will Go

F
The wheels go 'round and 'round.
(Arms move in a circular motion)

We drive the car in town.
(Drive like we're steering)

We buckle up
(Buckle seat belt)

In case we stop
(Hold out palm)

       C   F
So we'll be safe and sound.
(Cuddle ourselves)

      Judy Hall
      Wytheville, VA

Buckle Up

Sung to: Twinkle, Twinkle, Little Star

C   F   C
When I get in-to the car,

 G7   C   G7   C
I buckle up for near or far.

         G7   C   G7
It holds me in my seat so tight.

 C   G7   C   G7
I feel so safe; I know it's right.

   C   F   C
I use my seatbelt every day,

 G7   C   G7   C
So I'll be safe in every way.

      Susan Burbridge
      Beavercreek, OH

We Buckle Up

Sung to: When Johnny Comes Marching Home

      Em
We like to travel in our car,

      G
Hur-rah! Hurrah!

      Em
Our car can take us near or far,

      B
Hur-rah! Hurrah!

     G   D
We buckle up be-fore we go,

Em   B
Whether we're going fast or slow,

     Em Am Em B Em
So we'll all be saf-er riding in our car.

      Vicki Shannon
      Napton, MO

Safety—Buckle Up

1-57029-521-2 *Piggyback Songs—School Days*

I'm a Healthy Person

Sung to: I'm a Little Teapot

C
I'm a healthy person,

F   C
Walking down the street,
(Walk around room.)

G7   C
Swinging my arms

    G7   C
And stretching my feet.
(Swing arms and take big steps.)

I feel so good.

    F   C
My heart does, too.
(Point to heart.)

F
Walk with me—

    G7   C
It's good for you!

Jean Warren

A Toothbrush

Sung to: Yankee Doodle

    C
Of all the things a-round the town

           G
A toothbrush is a dandy.

    C
Brush up and down and all around,

  G   C
And stay away from candy.

Florence Dieckmann
Roanoke, VA

Wash, Wash, Wash Your Hands

Sung to: Row, Row, Row Your Boat

F
Wash, wash, wash your hands (face).

Wash them (it) day and night.

Soap and water does the trick.

It keeps them (it) clean and bright!

F
Brush, brush, brush your teeth.

Use some toothpaste, too!

Brush up and down and all around,

And eat what's right for you!

Judy Hall
Wytheville, VA

Hand Washing Time

Sung to: London Bridge

C
Here we go to wash our hands,

G   C
Wash our hands, wash our hands.

Here we go to wash our hands,

    G   C
Be-fore we eat our snack.

Substitute other activities for the phrase eat
our snack.

Cathy Griffin
Plainsboro, NJ

1-57029-521-2 *Piggyback Songs—School Days*

Health

Wash, Wash

Sung to: Ten Little Indians

C
Lava, lava tus manitas.
(Pretend to wash hands.)

G7
Lava, lava tu carita.
(Pretend to wash face.)

C
Lava, lava tus dientitos,
(Pretend to brush teeth.)

G7   C
Todas las ma-ñanas.

C
Peina, peina, tu cabello.
(Pretend to comb hair.)

G7
Ponte, ponte tu ropita.
(Pretend to put on clothes.)

C
Calza, calza tus zapatos,
(Pretend to put on shoes.)

G7   C
Todas las ma-ñanas.

New Eton School Staff

Spanish Pronunciation

LAH-vah, LAH-vah toos mah-NEE-tahs.
LAH-vah, LAH-vah too cah-REE-tah.
LAH-vah, LAH-vah toos dee-ehn-TEE-tohs,
TOH-dahs lahs mahn-YAHN-nahs.
PAY-nah, PAY-nah too kah-BAY-yoh.
POHN-tay, POHN-tay too roh-PEE-tah.
KAHL-sah, KAHL-sah toos sah-PAH-tohs,
TOH-dahs lahs mahn-YAH-nahs.

English Translation

Wash, wash your little hands.
Wash, wash your little face.
Brush, brush your little teeth,
Every morning.
Comb, comb your hair.
Put on, put on your little clothes.
Put on, put on your shoes,
Every morning.

Good Grooming

Sung to: The Mulberry Bush

D
This is the way we wash our face,

A
Wash our face, wash our face.

D
This is the way we wash our face,

   A   D
So early in the morning.

Use hand motions and add verses, using:
wash our hands; brush or teeth; comb our
hair; take a bath; put on our clothes, *etc.*

Lynn Beaird
Lompoc, CA

Health

Choose Foods That Are Good for You

Sung to: The Battle Hymn of the Republic

G
Choose foods that are good for you

At every meal you eat.

C
Choose foods that are good for you

   G
At every meal you eat.

Choose foods that are good for you

At every meal you eat,

   C   D7   G
And you'll grow up big and strong.

G
Breads and grains and fruits and veggies,

C   G
Meats and beans are good choices.

G
Milk and cheese and yogurt, also,

C   D7   G
Help you grow big and strong.

Priscilla M. Starrett
Warren, PA

Health Song

Sung to: Row, Row, Row Your Boat

C
Milk, meat, bread, and fruit,

These will help me grow,

To be strong and tall and well—

Healthy from head to toe.

Barbara Robinson
Huntington Beach, CA

Published by Totline Publications. Copyright protected.
1-57029-521-2 *Piggyback Songs—School Days*

So Many Parts of Me

Sung to: Twinkle, Twinkle, Little Star

| C | F | C |
On my face I have a nose.

| G7 | C | G7 | C |
On my feet I have ten toes.

| G7 | C | G7 |
I've five fingers on each hand.

| C | G7 | C | G7 |
I've two legs that help me stand.

| C | | F | C |
I have two eyes so I can see.

| G7 | C | G7 | C |
There are so many parts of me!

Diane Thom
Maple Valley, WA

Body Joints Song

Sung to: Frere Jacques

C
Find your elbows. Find your elbows.

Bend them now. This is how.
(Bend elbows.)

Elbows bend your arm bones.

Elbows bend your arm bones.

Bend them now. Bend them now.

C
Find your wrists. Find your wrists.

Bend them now. This is how.
(Bend wrists.)

Wrists bend your hand bones.

Wrists bend your hand bones.

Bend them now. Bend them now.

C
Find your knees. Find your knees.

Bend them now. This is how.
(Bend knees.)

Knees bend your leg bones.

Knees bend your leg bones.

Bend them now. Bend them now.

C
Find your ankles. Find your ankles.

Bend them now. This is how.
(Bend ankles.)

Ankles bend your foot bones.

Ankles bend your foot bones.

Bend them now. Bend them now.

Betty Silkunas
Lansdale, PA

Parts of the Body

1-57029-521-2 *Piggyback Songs—School Days*

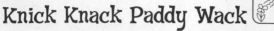

Knick Knack Paddy Wack

Sung to: This Old Man

C
This old man was a spy.

F
He played knick knack on my eye,

With a knick knack paddy wack

C
Give a dog a bone.

G7
This old man came rol-ling home.

Additional Verses:

This old man liked to doze.
He played knick knack on my nose.

This old man lived down south.
He played knick knack on my mouth.

This old man couldn't hear.
He played knick knack on my ear.

This old man liked to linger.
He played knick knack on my finger.

This old man went to the farm.
He played knick knack on my arm.

This old man ate a snack.
He played knick knack on my back.

This old man liked to beg.
He played knick knack on my leg.

Adapted Traditional

Head and Shoulders

Sung to: Frere Jacques

C
Head and shoulders, head and shoulders,

Knees and toes, knees and toes.

Head and shoulders, head and shoulders,

Knees and toes, knees and toes.

C
Eyes and ears, eyes and ears,

Mouth and nose, mouth and nose.

Eyes and ears, eyes and ears,

Mouth and nose, mouth and nose.

Adapted Traditional

Eyes and Ears

Sung to: Frere Jacques

C
Eyes and year, eyes and ears,

Mouth and nose, mouth and nose.

Can you see my eyes?

Can you see my ears?

And my mouth? And my nose?

Point to each body part mentioned as you sing the song.

Adapted Traditional

Parts of the Body

Eeny, Meeny, Miney, Mo

Sung to: This Old Man

C
Eeny, meeny, miney, mo,

F   G7
Catch (child's name) by the toe.

     C   F   C
And if (s/he) hollers let (him/her) go.

G7   C G7 C
Eeny, meeny, min-ey, mo.

   Adapted Traditional

Here We Go Looby Loo

C
Here we go looby loo,

              G7
Here we go looby light.

C
Here we go looby loo.

G7   C
All on a Saturday night.

     C
You put a hand in,

You take a hand out.

You give your hand a shake, shake, shake,

        G7   C
And turn your-self a-bout.

*Repeat chorus and second verse using a foot;
your head; whole self.*

   Adapted Traditional

This Is the Way

Sung to: London Bridge

C
This is the way we feel our muscles,

G   C
Feel our muscles, feel our muscles.

This is the way we feel our muscles,

G   C
Right before we punch. *(Pretend to punch.)*

C
This is the way we use our lungs,

G   C
Use our lungs, use our lungs.

C
This is the way we use our lungs,

   G   C
To blow out birthday candles.
(Blow out candles.)

C
This is the way we feel our hearts,

G   C
Feel our hearts, feel our hearts.

This is the way we feel our hearts

G   C
Beating up and down, thump-thump . . .
(Feel hearts.)

   Valerie Bielsker
   Overland Park, KS

Parts of the Body

 1-57029-521-2 *Piggyback Songs—School Days*

Show Me If You Can

Sung to: Go In and Out the Window

F   C
Whe-ere is your finger?

             F
Whe-ere is your finger?

             C
Whe-ere is your finger?

             F
Show me if you can.

F   C
Good, now where's your nose?

             F
Now, where is your nose?

             C
Now, where is your nose?

             F
Show me if you can.

Continue with other body parts.

Barbara Robinson
Glendale, AZ

Put Your Finger on Your Nose

Sung to: If You're Happy and You Know It

C   G7
Put your finger on your nose, on your nose.

                  C
Put your finger on your nose, on your nose.

           F
Put your finger on your nose,

      C
And feel it as it grows.

      G7   C
Put your finger on your nose, on your nose.

      C   G7
Put your finger on your toe, on your toe.

                  C
Put your finger on your toe, on your toe.

           F
Put your finger on your toe,

      C
And move it to and fro.

      G7   C
Put your finger on your toe, on your toe.

      C   G7
Put your finger on your ear, on your ear.

                  C
Put your finger on your ear, on your ear.

           F
Put your finger on your ear,

      C
And see if it's still here.

      G7   C
Put your finger on your ear, on your ear.

Make up other verses about different body parts.

Jean Warren

Parts of the Body

98

1-57029-521-2 *Piggyback Songs—School Days*

I Am Special

Sung to: London Bridge

C
I am special. Yes, I am,

G   C
Yes, I am, yes, I am.

C
I am special. Yes, I am.

G   C
I'm very special.

C
No one else has hair like mine—

G   C
Just like mine, just like mine.

C
No one else has hair like mine.

G   C
I'm very special.

C
No one else has a face like mine—

G   C
Just like mine, just like mine.

C
No one else has a face like mine.

G   C
I'm very special.

C
No one else has eyes like mine—

G   C
Just like mine, just like mine.

C
No one else has eyes like mine.

G   C
I'm very special.

(Use nose, mouth, etc.)

Judy Bush
Franklin, MA

You Can, Too

Sung to: Frere Jacques

C
Laura is painting. Laura is painting.

You can, too. You can, too.

She's painting red and yellow.

She's painting red and yellow.

You can, too. You can, too.

C
Jacob is building. Jacob is building.

You can, too. You can, too.

He's building with the blocks.

He's building with the blocks.

You can, too. You can, too.

Substitute the names of your children and the things that they are doing for those in the song.

Gayle Bittinger

1-57029-521-2 *Piggyback Songs—School Days*

Self-Esteem—Special

Special Me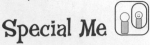

Sung to: Twinkle, Twinkle, Little Star

C   F   C
Special, special, special me.
(Point to self.)

G7   C   G7   C
How I wonder what I'll be.
(Rest chin on folded hands.)

        G7   C   G7
In the big world I can be
(Make circle with arms.)

C G7 C   G7
Any-thing I want to be.
(Nod head.)

C   F   C
Special, special, special me.
(Point to self.)

G7   C   G7   C
How I wonder what I'll be.
(Rest chin on folded hands.)

Kristine Wagoner
Puyallup, WA

You Are Special

Sung to: Frere Jacques

C
You are special. You are special.

That's for sure. That's for sure.

No one else is like you.

No one else is like you.

You're our friend. You're our friend.

Sing the song for each of your children.

Laura Egge
Lake Oswego, OR

A Special Person

Sung to: Jimmy Crack Corn

F   C7
Alan is a special person.

         F
Alan is a special person.

         B♭
Alan is a special person.

      C7   F
And that's why we like him.

*Sing the song for each of your children,
substituting the child's name for* Alan.

Laura Egge
Lake Oswego, OR

Mirror, Mirror

Sung to: Twinkle, Twinkle, Little Star

C   F   C
I look in the mirror and who do I see?
(Pretend to look in a mirror.)

  G7 C   G7   C
A very wonderful, special me!
(Point to self.)

     C   G7   C   G7
With sparkling eyes all shiny and bright,
(Point to eyes.)

     C   G7   C   G7
My smile shows my teeth so pearly white.
(Show teeth in a smile.)

     C   F   C
It certainly is great to be
(Nod head.)

  G7 C   G7   C
This very wonderful, special me!
(Hug self.)

Ann M. O'Connell
Coaldale, PA

Published by Totline Publications. Copyright protected.

1-57029-521-2 *Piggyback Songs—School Days*

Super Star

Sung to: The Muffin Man

    F
Oh, do you know a super star,

 G7   C
A super star, a super star?

    F
Oh, yes, I know a super star.

   G7   C   F
The super star is me!

       Paula Laughtland
       Edmonds, WA

All About Me

Sung to: Twinkle, Twinkle, Little Star

C   F   C
Let me tell you all about me.

G7 C   G7   C
I am special, you will see.

     G7   C   G7
I can count and run and sing.

C   G7   C G7
I can do most any-thing.

C   F   C
Let me tell you all about me.

G7 C   G7   C
I am special, you will see.

*Repeat, encouraging your children to
substitute their special talents for* count, run,
and sing.

       Betty Silkunas
       Lansdale, PA

✓ So Many People Love You

Sung to: Did You Ever See a Lassie?

     F
So many people love you.

    C7   F
They love you. They love you.

So many people love you.

    C7   F
They love you so much—

    C7   F
Like Mommy and Daddy

    C7   F
And Grandma and Grandpa.

     F
So many people love you.

    C7   F
They love you so much.

*Repeat, substituting names your children
suggest for* Mommy, Daddy, Grandma, *and*
Grandpa.

       Laura Egge
       Lake Oswego, OR

Self-Esteem

I Know How

Sung to: If You're Happy and You Know It

      F   C
Oh, I know how to put on my own shoes.
(Pretend to put on shoes.)

                          F
I can put on my own shirt. Yes, it's true.
(Pretend to put on shirt.)

           B♭
I know how to wash my face,
(Pretend to wash face.)

                F
And comb my hair back into place.
(Pretend to comb hair.)

  C   F
Oh, look at all the things that I can do!

Becky Valenick
Rockford, IL

What I Do Best

Sung to: Twinkle, Twinkle, Little Star

C   F   C
What thing can you do the best?

G7   C   G7   C
Help us all so we can guess!

          G7   C   G7
Can you lead or can you read?

C   G7   C   G7
Can you sing or pump a swing?

C   F   C
Tell us, tell us, tell us, do.

G7   C   G7 C
Please, oh, please, give us a clue.

Janice Bodenstedt
Jackson, MI

You Can Do It

Sung to: London Bridge

    C
If you want to learn something new,

G7   C
Something new, something new—

If you want to learn something new,

G7   C
Keep on trying!

C
If you practice, you will see,

G7   C
You will see, you will see—

If you practice, you will see

G7   C
You can do it!

Janice Bodenstedt
Jackson, MI

I Like It

Sung to: A-Tisket, A-Tasket

C
I like it. I like it.

I like the way you did that.

      G7
You put the toys back in the box.

                C
I like the way you did it.

Substitute an appropriate phrase, such as you zipped your coat up by yourself, or you painted with the purple paint, for you put the toys back on the box.

Laura Egge
Lake Oswego, OR

1-57029-521-2 *Piggyback Songs—School Days*

Self-Esteem—Look What You Can Do

How I Feel

Sung to: Twinkle, Twinkle, Little Star

C   F   C
Sometimes on my face you'll see

G7   C   G7   C
How I feel in-side of me.

              G7   C   G7
A smile means happy, a frown means sad.

     C   G7   C   G7
And when I grit my teeth I'm mad.

C   F   C
When I'm proud, I beam and glow,

    G7   C   G7   C
But when I'm shy, my head hangs low.

> Karen Folk
> Franklin, MA

Tell Me How You Feel

Sung to: Skip to My Lou

F
Show me how you look when you're mad.

C7
Show me how you look when you're sad.

F
Show me how you look when you're glad.

    C7   F
Then tell me how you feel now.

Sing the song for each of your children.

> Laura Egge
> Lake Oswego, OR

Tears, Tears, Go Away

Sung to: Rain, Rain, Go Away

C
Tears, tears, go away;

Come again some other day.

G
Tears, tears, go away;

                       C
Little (child's name) wants to play.

> Sister Linda Kaman, R.S.M.
> Pittsburgh, PA

When You're Sad

Sung to: Twinkle, Twinkle, Little Star

C   F   C
Sometimes when I'm feeling sad,

 G7   C   G7   C
I think of Mom and I think of Dad.

          G7   C   G7
I think of all the things they do

     C   G7   C   G7
To try and help me not be blue.

     C   F   C
So when you're sad and all a-lone,

G7   C   G7   C
Think of all you have at home.

> Barbara Robinson
> Huntington Beach, CA

1-57029-521-2 *Piggyback Songs—School Days*

Happy Faces

Sung to: Jingle Bells

F
Smiling faces, happy faces,

Giggling all around.

C7   F
Oh, what fun we'll have this way

   G7   C7
In a happy class to-day.

F
He-he-he, he-he-he,

He-he-he-he-he.

C7   F
Ha-ha-ha, ha-ha-ha-ha,

   C7   F
In a happy class to-day!

     Susan Peters
     Upland, CA

S-M-I-L-E

Sung to: Don't Sit Under the Apple Tree

  C
It isn't any trouble just S-M-I-L-E,

G7   C
S-M-I-L-E, S-M-I-L-E.

It isn't any trouble just to S-M-I-L-E,

    G7   C
If you only take the trouble just to S-M-I-L-E.

     Linda Robinson
     Centerville, MA

Are You Smiling?

Sung to: Frere Jacques

C
Are you smiling? Are you smiling?

I like you! I like you!

This is such a nice place

For a sunny, bright face.

I like you! I like you!

     Mildred Hoffman
     Tacoma, WA

Love

Sung to: Row, Row, Row Your Boat

F
Love, love is all around.

It will grow with you.

Show it, tell it, feel it, share it.

Make it part of you.

     Adele Engelbracht
     River Ridge, LA

Feelings

104 1-57029-521-2 *Piggyback Songs—School Days*

Good Manners Is Thinking of Others

Sung to: My Bonnie Lies Over the Ocean

    C   F   C
"Good manners" means thinking of others.

               D7   G
"Good manners" means doing what's right.

    C   F   C
"Good manners" means thinking of others.

     F   G   C
Good manners always feel right.

C   F
Helping, caring,

G   C
Sharing with you to-day, today.

        F
Kindness, honesty,

G   C
Sharing with you to-day.

    Susan Peters
    Upland, CA

Manners

Sung to: Hickory, Dickory, Dock

C   G   C
Cover your mouth when you cough.

       G   C
Cover your mouth when you sneeze.

     G   C   G
If you cough or if you sneeze—

C   G   C
Cover your mouth, if you please.

    Ruth Miller
    San Antonio, TX

Learning Manners

Sung to: The Camptown Races

F
Learning manners can be fun;

C
Please and thank you.

F
"Yes, ma'am" and "no, sir" are some,

C   G
Say them every day.

When we learn them well,

B♭   F
You can always tell.

Pardon me. You're welcome, too.

    C   F
Use manners every day.

    Judy Hall
    Wytheville, VA

Manners Are the Way

Sung to: The Farmer in the Dell

F
Manners are the way

To brighten up my day.

Please and thank you's what I say

G   F
To brighten up my day.

    Becky Valenick
    Rockford, IL

Manners

Please and Thank You

Sung to: The Muffin Man

F
Please and thank you; how are you?

  G7   C7
Po-lite words will always do.

F
Friends feel good, and you will, too.

G7   F
I can use them. How 'bout you?

      Bev Qualheim
      Marquette, MI

These Little Words

Sung to: London Bridge

     C
These little words can make you smile,

G7   C
Make you smile, make you smile.

These little words can make you smile—

G7   C
Please and thank you.

      Betty Silkunas
      Lansdale, PA

Talking to People

Sung to: Did You Ever See a Lassie?

              F
When you talk to people,

   C7   F
You should use good manners.

When you talk to people,

   C7   F
You should be po-lite.

    C7   F
When they say, "Thank you,"

    C7   F
Then you say, "You're welcome."

When you talk to people,

   C7   F
You should be po-lite.

              F
When you talk to people,

   C7   F
You should use good manners.

When you talk to people,

   C7   F
You should be po-lite.

    C7   F
When they say, "How are you?"

    C7   F
Then you say, "Fine, thank you."

When you talk to people,

   C7   F
You should be po-lite.

      Jean D. Smith
      Huron, OH

Please and Thank You

Sung to: Frere Jacques

C
Por favor, por favor,

If you please, if you please.

Thank you very much.

Thank you very much.

Muchas gracias, muchas gracias.

Sue St. John

Spanish Pronunciation

Pohr fah-VOHR, pohr fah-VOHR,
If you please, if you please.
Thank you very much.
Thank you very much.
MOO-chahs GRAH-see-ahs,
MOO-chahs GRAH-see-ahs.

English Translation

Please, please,
If you please, if you please.
Thank you very much.
Thank you very much.
Many thanks, many thanks.

Kind Words

Sung to: Skip to My Lou

F
It's nice to say, "Thank you."

C7
It's nice to say, "Thank you."

F
It's nice to say, "Thank you."

C7
When someone's kind to you.

F
It's nice to say, "Excuse me."

C7
It's nice to say, "Excuse me."

F
It's nice to say, "Excuse me."

C7   F
When you cough or sneeze.

F
It's nice to say, "Please."

C7
It's nice to say, "Please."

F
It's nice to say, "Please,"

C7   F
When you ask for help.

Judith Taylor Burtchet
El Dorado, KS

Manners—Polite Words

Share Our Toys

Sung to: Row, Row, Row Your Boat

C
Let's all share our toys.

Let's share them with our friends.

It's so much fun to share our toys.

Sharing has no end.

> Rosemary Giordano
> Philadelphia, PA

We Share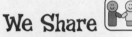

Sung to: Twinkle, Twinkle, Little Star

C   F   C
We share all our blocks and toys

G7 C G7   C
With the other girls and boys.

    G7   C   G7
Crayons, scissors, paint and glue,

C G7   C G7
Puzzles, books, the easel, too.

C   F   C
We take turns be-cause it's fair,

G7   C G7   C
And we're happy when we share.

> Sue Brown
> Louisville, KY

Sharing

Sung to: Row, Row, Row Your Boat

C
Share, share, share the toys.

It's so much fun to share.

I share with you; you share with me.

We share because we care.

> Elizabeth McKinnon

Manners—Sharing

Taking Turns

Sung to: Mary Had a Little Lamb

C
On the playground please take turns,

G7   C
Please take turns, please take turns.

Remember others like a turn,

   G7   C
And always try to share.

      Patricia Coyne
      Mansfield, MA

Cooperation

Sung to: Yankee Doodle

C   G7
Cooperation is the thing

   C   G7
We all must learn to do.

C   F
It makes life so very nice

   G7   C
And gets the work done, too.

F
Let's cooperate today

C
In our work and play.

F
Who knows what we can get done

   C   G7   C
If we all work this way!

      Jean Warren

We Are Helpers

Sung to: This Old Man

C
We are pals as we play,

F   G7
Helpers sharing every day,

        C
With a, "May I help?" and a "Thank you," too.

G7   C   G7 C
We are helpers through and through.

      Margery A. Kranyik
      Hyde Park, MA

We Know How to Get Along

Sung to: Mary Had a Little Lamb

C
We know how to get along,

G7   C
Get along, get along.

We know how to get along

G7   C
Every single day.

C
We take turns and share a lot,

G7   C
Share a lot, share a lot.

We take turns and share a lot

G7   C
While we work and play.

      Kathy McCullough
      St. Charles, IL

1-57029-521-2 *Piggyback Songs—School Days*

Manners—Getting Along

✓ Together

Sung to: Did You Ever See a Lassie?

     F
The more we learn together,

 C7   F
to-gether, to-gether,

The more we learn together,

    C7   F
the happier we'll be.

    C7   F
For my school is your school,

   C7   F
And your school is my school.

The more we learn together,

    C7   F
the happier we'll be.

     F
The more we share together,

   C7   F
to-gether, to-gether,

The more we share together,

    C7   F
the happier we'll be.

   C7   F
For my toys are your toys,

    C7   F
And your toys are my toys.

The more we share together,

   C7   F
the happier we'll be.

    F   C7   F
The more we play together, to-gether, to-gether,

                      C7   F
The more we play together, the happier we'll be.

   C7   F
For my friends are your friends,

   C7   F
And your friends are my friends.

                      C7   F
The more we play together, the happier we'll be.

    F   C7   F
The more we smile together, to-gether, to-gether,

                      C7   F
The more we smile together, the happier we'll be.

   C7   F
For my smile's a big smile,

   C7   F
And your smile's a big smile.

                      C7   F
The more we smile together, the happier we'll be.

Margery A. Kranyik
Hyde Park, MA

Friend

Interlock right and left index fingers, then separate hands and interlock again in opposite positions.

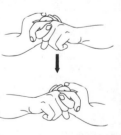

Friends

Friends 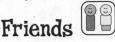 ✓

Sung to: ABC Song

C   F   C
Friends are big, and friends are small.

G7   C   G7   C
Friends will help you if you fall.

C   G7   C   G7
Friends are happy; friends are sad.

C   G7   C   G7
Friends can make each other glad.

C   F   C
Friends are short, and friends are tall.

G7   C   G7   C
Friends are happy when you call.

C   F   C
Friends are young and friends are old.

G7   C   G7   C
Friends are worth much more than gold.

      G7   C   G7
Friends are near and friends are far.

C   G7   C   G7
Friends will like you as you are.

C   F   C
Friends are dark, and friends are light.

G7   C   G7   C
Friends will bring you much de-light!

   Jean Warren

All Our Friends

Sung to: The Camptown Races

C
All our friends are here today,

G7
Hooray! Hooray!

C
All our friends are here today,

G7   C
Here to work and play.

Friends can help us smile

F   C
All along the way.

I'll be your friend, and you'll be mine.

G7   C
Happy, happy day!

    Margery A Kranyik
    Hyde Park, MA

New Friends

Sung to: Oh, What a Beautiful Morning

C   B♭ F
Hello, new friend, how are you?

C   G7
Hello, new friend of mine.

C   F   F#dim
I am so glad that I met you;

C   G7   C
New friends are hard to find!

    Jean Warren

1-57029-521-2 Piggyback Songs—School Days

Friends

Sung to: Jack and Jill

```
     G     C           G        C
I have a friend; (her/his) name is _____,

      G              C  G
And we have fun to-ge-ther.

       Am                  G
We laugh and play and sing all day,

     Am         D7  G
In any kind of  wea-ther.
```

Ruth Miller
San Antonio, TX

With All My Friends

Sung to: She'll Be Coming 'Round the Mountain

```
       F
Oh, I like to go to school with all my friends.

                                    C7
Oh, I like to go to school with all my friends.

       F
There is Tonya, Luis, Eric,

        B♭
And there's Keisha, Garth, and Emily.

     F          C7              F
Oh, I like to go to school with all my friends.
```

Substitute the names of your children for those in the song and repeat until each child has been mentioned.

Barbara Backer
Charleston, SC

Counting Friends

Sung to: London Bridge

```
C
How many friends are here today,

G7           C
Here to work, here to play?

How many friends are here today?

G7        C
Let's all count them.
(Count.)
```

Betty Silkunas
Lansdale, PA

Be My Friend

Sung to: Mary Had a Little Lamb

```
C
Will you come and play with me,

G           C
Play with me, play with me?

C
Will you come and play with me?

G           C
Please be my friend.
```

Betty Ruth Baker
Waco, TX

1-57029-521-2 *Piggyback Songs—School Days*

We're Friends Already

Sung to: The Bear Went Over the Mountain

C
Hoy nos conocimos,

G7
Hoy nos conocimos,

Hoy nos conocimos,

    C   G7   C
¡Y amigos somos ya!

Sonya Kranwinkel

Spanish
Pronunciation

Oy nohs koh-noh-SEE-mohs,
Oy nohs koh-noh-SEE-mohs,
Oy nohs koh-noh-SEE-mohs,
Ee ah-MEE-gohs SOH-mohs yah!

English Translation

Today we met,
Today we met,
Today we met,
And we are friends already!

I Have a Friend

Sung to: The Mulberry Bush

D
I have a friend who plays with me,

A7
Plays with me, plays with me.

D
I have a friend who plays with me.

A7   D
Here's what we like to do.

D
We like to stack the blocks up high,

A7
Blocks up high, blocks up high.

D
We like to stack the blocks up high.

A7   D
That's what we like to do.

D
We like to play with the big dump truck,

A7
Big dump truck, big dump truck.

D
We like to play with the big dump truck.

                     D
That's what we like to do.

Continue with similar verses about things your children like to do with their friends.

Elizabeth McKinnon

1-57029-521-2 *Piggyback Songs—School Days*

Friends

Oh Where, Oh Where Have My Helpers Gone?

Sung to: Oh, Where, Oh Where Has My Little Dog Gone?

D   A7
Oh where, oh where have my helpers gone?

                 D
I need some help right a-way.

             A7
I don't want to do this job alone.

                 D
Oh, helpers, please come my way!

Laura Egge
Lake Oswego, OR

Helping

Sung to: Sing a Song of Sixpence

C   G7
Being a good helper is very fun to do.

It makes someone happy

   C
And makes me happy, too.

C
When the job is finished,

C7
They will say,

    F
"Thank you."

G7
And I will say "You're welcome.

          C
I am glad I could help you."

Diana Nazaruk
Clark Lake, MI

Need Our Helpers

Sung to: Oh, My Darling Clementine

F
Need our helpers, need our helpers,

                  C7
Need our helpers to-day.

                        F
Time for helpers to do their jobs,

        C7   F
Need our helpers to-day.

F
Water plants, water plants,

                  C7
Water plants so they grow strong.

                    F
Time to water our nice plants,

        C7   F
Need our helpers to-day.

F
Pass our papers, pass out papers,

                  C7
Pass out papers to our class.

                    F
Please help me pass out papers,

        C7   F
Need our helpers to-day.

Create your own verses as needed.

Cindy Dingwall
Palatine, IL

1-57029-521-2 *Piggyback Songs—School Days*

I'm a Helper

Sung to: London Bridge

C
I'm a helper; yes, I am,

G   C
Yes, I am; yes, I am.

I'm a helper; yes, I am.

G   C
I'm a helper.

C
I will close the door today,

G   C
Door today, door today.

I will close the door today.

G   C
I'm a helper.

Additional Verses: I will be the leader today; I
will turn on the lights today; I will feed the fish
today; I will mark the calendar today; etc.

> Rita Galloway
> Harlingen, TX

All Day Long

Sung to: Mary Had a Little Lamb

C
Molly is in charge of blocks,

  G7   C
In charge of blocks, in charge of blocks.

Molly is in charge of blocks,

G7   C
All day long.

*Substitute one of your children's names for the
name* Molly, *and the appropriate job for the
phrase* in charge of blocks.

> Ann-Marie Donovan
> Framingham, MA

Thanks for All You Do

Sung to: Yankee Doodle

C   G7
Thanks for all you do for us,

C   G7
Mr. Green, you're spe-cial.

  C   F
You helped us with our work and play.

G7   C
Thank you, Mr. Green.

F
You are special to us all;

  C
We needed you so much.

  F
We know you care and give your time.

  C   G7 C
We love you, Mr. Green.

*Substitute the name of one of your school
helpers for the name* Mr. Green.

> Patricia Coyne
> Mansfield, MA

1-57029-521-2 *Piggyback Songs—School Days*

Helpers

Community Helpers Song

Sung to: Rudolph the Red-Nosed Reindeer

C
Mail carriers bring mail;

C   G7
Nurses help us when we're sick.

G7
Bankers deposit money.

G7   C
Farmers raise cows, goats, and chicks.

F   C   C7
Doctors, teachers, and police—

Dm   G7   C
We all need them so.

G
Each does his important part—

Am   D7   G
Always on the go.

C
Bus drivers, sales, and fire fighters—

                              G7
Couldn't do without them too!

G7
Can't wait 'til you grow up.

                              C
There are so many jobs for you!

> Barb Robinson
> Huntington Beach, CA

Police and Fire Fighters

Sung to: I'm a Little Teapot

C
I am a peace officer, with my star.

G7
I help people near and far.

C
If you have a problem, call on me.

And I will be there, 1, 2, 3!

C   F   C
I'm a fire fighter, dressed in red

G7   C   G7   C
With my fire hat on my head.

C   F   C
I can drive the fire truck, fight fires, too,

        F   C   G   G7 C
And help to make things safe for you.

> Judy Hall
> Wytheville, VA

To the Hospital

Sung to: Frere Jacques

F
To the hospital, to the hospital,

We will go, we will go.

We will see the doctors.

We will see the nurses,

Dressed in white, dressed in white.

> Karen Pound
> Webster City, IA

1-57029-521-2 *Piggyback Songs—School Days*

Community Helpers

Who Are We?

Sung to: I've Been Working on the Railroad

G
We've been working in the kitchen,

C   G
All the live long day.

We've been working in the kitchen,

      A7   D
Making food along the way.

D7   G
When you hear that it is lunchtime,

C   B7
You'll know what we mean.

C   G
All the food that we've been making

      D7   G
Is the best you've ever seen.

(Who are we?)

G
We've been working in the office,

C   G
All the live long day.

We've been working in the office,

          A7   D
Answering phones along the way.

D7   G
When you're feeling kind of sickly,

C   B7
You will come to us.

C   G
We will call your mommy,

          D7 G
All with-out a fuss.

(Who are we?)

Judy Hall
Wytheville, VA

Firefighters

Sung to: Pop Goes the Weasel

C   G   C
Down the street the engine goes.

  C   G C
The brave fire-fighters.

C   G   C
Up the ladder with their hose—

F   G   C
Out goes the fire.

Mrs. Gary McNitt
Adrian, MI

Today's Helpers

Sung to: The Mulberry Bush

C   G
(Todd) will be the helper today, helper today,
    helper today.

C   G
(Todd) will be the helper today, he will put
              C
    the blocks away.

Substitute the name of one of your children
for the name Todd, *and the appropriate job for*
the phrase put the blocks away.

Barbara Paxson
Warren, OH

 1-57029-521-2 *Piggyback Songs—School Days*

Concepts

Color Foods

Sung to: Mary Had a Little Lamb

C
I can eat a food that's red:

G7   C
Good to eat, what a treat!

A food that's red is a strawberry.

G7   C
Yum, yum, yum, yum, yum.

*Sing the song for each of your children,
letting the child choose the color and food
he or she wants to sing about.*

Barbara Backer
Charleston, SC

Colors That We Know

Sung to: Twinkle, Twinkle, Little Star

C   F   C
Yellow sunshine, soft green grass,

G7   C   G7   C
Orange goldfish, small black bats.

C   G7   C   G7
Blue cold water, purple plums,

C   G7   C   G7
Red straw-berries—yum, yum, yum!

C   F   C
Big brown tree trunks, bright white snow.

G7   C   G7   C
These are colors that we know.

Diane Thom
Maple Valley, WA

1-57029-521-2 *Piggyback Songs—School Days*

○ ○ ○ 1 2 3 ◇ □ ◻ A B C ☆ ★ ☆ a b c

Five Colors Song

Sung to: Three Blind Mice

✓ C
Red, red, red. Red, red, red.

What is red? What is red?

An apple, a rose, and a strawberry,

Cherries growing on a tree,

My nose on a day that's cold and frosty—

They all are red.

✓ C
Yellow, yellow, yellow. Yellow, yellow, yellow.

What is yellow? What is yellow?

A school bus parked at the school bus stop,

Bananas grown in a land that's hot,

Daffodils bright in a garden spot—

They all are yellow.

✓ C
Blue, blue, blue. Blue, blue, blue.

What is blue? What is blue?

The sea, the sky, and some people's eyes,

Blueberries picked for a scrumptious pie,

A bluebird flying a-way up high—

They all are blue.

C
Green, green, green. Green, green, green.

What is green? What is green?

Grass and plants and trees and leaves,

Lettuce we put in the salad we eat,

Grasshoppers hopping around our feet—

They all are green.

C
Orange, orange, orange. Orange, orange, orange.

What is orange? What is orange?

An orange, a cantaloupe, and a peach,

A pumpkin, a goldfish, and Cheddar cheese,

The carrot that my little rabbit eats—

They all are orange.

Diane Thom
Maple Valley, WA

Colors

Colors

Sung to: Frere Jacques

C
Red is rojo; green is verde;

Blue, azul; negro, black;

Yellow, amarillo;

Purple is morado;

Gray is gris; brown, café.

New Eton School Staff

Spanish Pronunciation

Red is ROH-hoh; green is VEHR-day;
Blue, ah-SOOL; NEH-groh, black;
Yellow, ah-mah-REE-yoh;
Purple is moh-RAH-doh;
Gray is grees; brown, kah-FAY.

English Translation

Red is red; green is green;
Blue, blue; black, black;
Yellow, yellow;
Purple is purple;
Gray is gray; brown, brown.

Rainbow Colors

Sung to: Hush, Little Baby

F   C7
Rainbow purple, rainbow blue,

                          F
Rainbow green and yellow, too.

                          C7
Rainbow orange and rainbow red,

                     F
Rainbow smiling overhead.

F   C7
Come and count the colors with me.

                     F
How many colors can you see?

                C7
One, two, three, down to green,

                          F
Four, five, six colors can be seen.

F   C7
Rainbow purple, rainbow blue,

                          F
Rainbow green and yellow, too.

                     C7
Rainbow orange and rainbow red,

                     F
Rainbow smiling overhead.

Jean Warren

Colors

○ ○ ● ○ 1 2 3 ◇ ▢ ◻ A B C ☆ ★ ☆ a b c

Where Are  the Colors?

Sung to: The Paw Paw Patch

F
Where, oh, where are the kids with blue on?

C7
Where, oh, where are the kids with blue on?

F
Where, oh, where are the kids with blue on?

C7   F
Stand up tall so we can see you now.

Repeat, each time substituting a different color for blue *and a different action for* stand up tall.

Ann-Marie Donovan
Framingham, MA

Colors

Sung to: The Farmer in the Dell

F
Oh, Mary is wearing blue.

Oh, Mary is wearing blue.

Heigh-ho the derry oh,

      C   F
Mary is wearing blue.

Continue using children's names and other colors.

Diana Nazaruk
Clark Lake, MI

If Your Clothes Have Any Red

Sung to: If You're Happy and You Know It

C   G7
If your clothes have any red, any red,

                       C
If your clothes have any red, any red,

           F   C
If your clothes have any red, put your finger
    on your head,

   G7   C
If your clothes have any red, any red.

C   G7
If your clothes have any blue, any blue,

                       C
If your clothes have any blue, any blue,

       F   C
If your clothes have any blue, put your finger
    on your shoe,

   G7   C
If your clothes have any blue, any blue.

Additional Verses: If your clothes have any green, wave your hand so you are seen; If your clothes have any yellow, smile like a happy fellow; If your clothes have any brown, turn your smile into a frown; If your clothes have any black, put your hands behind your back.

Jean Warren
Adapted Traditional

1-57029-521-2 *Piggyback Songs—School Days*

Colors—Wearing Colors

If You're Wearing Red Today

Sung to: If You're Happy and You Know It

    F   C
If you're wearing red today, nod your head.

                                  F
If you're wearing red today, nod your head.

    B♭
If you're wearing red today,

    F
Nod your head and shout hooray.

    C   F
If you're wearing red today, nod your head.

Additional Verses: If you're wearing blue today, tap your toe; If you're wearing yellow today, raise your hand; If you're wearing orange today, clap your hands; If you're wearing green today, stand up tall; If you're wearing purple today, turn around.

June Meckel
Andover, MA

If You Are Wearing Red

Sung to: If You're Happy and You Know It

    G   D
If you are wearing red, shake your head;

                               G
If you are wearing red, shake your head;

    C
If you are wearing red,

    G
Then please shake your head.

    D   G
If you are wearing red, shake your head.

Additional Verses: If you are wearing blue, touch your shoe; If you are wearing black, pat your back; If you are wearing green, bow like a queen; If you are wearing yellow, shake like Jell-O®; If you are wearing brown, turn around; If you are wearing pink, give us a wink; etc.

Janice Bodenstedt
Jackson, MI

The Color Song

Sung to: The Farmer in the Dell

    D
If you are wearing blue,

If you are wearing blue,

Stand up tall and turn around

    A7   D
And then sit right back down.

Repeat with other colors.

Ann-Marie Donovan
Framingham, MA

Published by Totline Publications. Copyright protected.

1-57029-521-2 *Piggyback Songs—School Days*

Color Song

Sung to: Twinkle, Twinkle, Little Star
(Alternating A, B, A, B, A sections)

C   F   C
Put your red shape in the air.

G7   C   G7   C
Hold it high and leave it there.

       G7   C   G7
Put your red shape on your back.

C   G7 C   G7
Now please lay it in your lap.

C   F   C
Hold your red shape in your hand.

G7   C G7   C
Now will every-one please stand.

      G7   C   G7
Wave your red shape at the door.

C   G7 C   G7
Now please lay it on the floor.

C   F   C
Hold your red shape and jump, jump, jump.

G7   C   G7   C
Throw your red shape way, way up.

*Substitute different colors. (Cut several shapes
from different colors of construction paper.
Great for recognizing colors, shapes, and
direction.)*

> Trish Peckham
> Raleigh, NC

Yellow Balloons

Sung to: Frere Jacques

C
Yellow balloons, yellow balloons,

Floating up, floating up,

Never let them touch the ground.

Never let them touch the ground.

Keep them up. Keep them up.

*Have the children pretend to keep balloons up
in the air as you sing the song. Sing the song
as many times as desired, letting the children
suggest other balloon colors.*

> Joyce Marshall
> Whitby, ON

Pretty Balloons

Sung to: Twinkle, Twinkle, Little Star

C   F   C
Pretty balloons in the air,

G7   C   G7   C
Lots of colors we see there.

       G7   C   G7
Red and yellow, green and blue—

C   G7   C   G7
Can you see the colors, too?

C   F   C
Pretty balloons in the air,

G7   C   G7   C
Lots of colors we see there.

> Susan Burbridge
> Beavercreek, OH

1-57029-521-2 *Piggyback Songs—School Days*

Colors—Activities

✓ ○ ○ ○ ○ 1 2 3 ◇ □ ◇ A B C ☆ ☆ ☆ a b c

Black and White
Sung to: Twinkle, Twinkle, Little Star

C   F C
Mixing black and white to-day,

G7 C G7 C
We will make the color gray:

    G7 C G7
Gray like concrete for the street,

C G7 C G7
Gray like clay or elephant feet.

C   F C
Mixing black and white to-day,

G7 C G7 C
We will make the color gray.

  Diane Thom
  Maple Valley, WA

Red and Blue
Sung to: Twinkle, Twinkle, Little Star

C   F C
Red and blue, red and blue:

G7 C G7 C
Mix them up, there's purple for you—

    G7 C G7
Purple like cabbage we sometimes eat,

C G7 C G7
Purple like plums that taste so sweet.

C   F C
Red and blue, red and blue:

G7 C G7 C
Mix them up, there's purple for you.

  Diane Thom
  Maple Valley, WA

Blue and Yellow
Sung to: If You're Happy and You Know It

    F   C
Blue and yellow mixed together will make green,

               F
Like the grass or a skinny, long string bean,

    B♭
Like a pickle or a lime.

    F
Yes, I promise every time,

    C   F
If you mix blue and yellow, you'll make green.

  Diane Thom
  Maple Valley, WA

Yellow and Red
Sung to: Twinkle, Twinkle, Little Star

C   F C
Yellow and red, yellow and red:

G7 C G7 C
Mix them—orange is what you'll get.

    G7 C G7
Orange is the color of a fruit you eat

C G7 C G7
Or a con-struction cone in the street.

C   F C
Yellow and red, yellow and red:

G7 C G7 C
Mix them—orange is what you'll get.

  Diane Thom
  Maple Valley, WA

Colors—Mixing

124

1-57029-521-2 *Piggyback Songs—School Days*

Shapes

Sung to: Frere Jacques

C
This is a square. This is a square.

How can you tell? How can you tell?

It has four sides

All the same size.

It's a square. It's a square.

C
This is a circle. This is a circle.

How can you tell? How can you tell?

It goes 'round and 'round.

No end can be found.

It's a circle. It's a circle.

C
This is a triangle. This is a triangle.

How can you tell? How can you tell?

It only has three sides

That join to make three points.

It's a triangle. It's a triangle.

C
This is a rectangle. This is a rectangle.

How can you tell? How can you tell?

It has two short sides,

And it has two long sides.

It's a rectangle. It's a rectangle.

Jeanne Petty
Camden, DE

Do You Know Its Name?

Sung to: Mary Had a Little Lamb

C
Do you know what shape this is,
(Hold up a triangle.)

G7   C
Shape this is, shape this is?

Do you know what shape this is?

G7   C
Do you know its name?

C
Yes, I know what shape it is,

G7   C
Shape it is, shape it is.

Yes, I know what shape it is.

G7   C
It is a trian-gle.

Betty Ruth Baker
Waco, TX

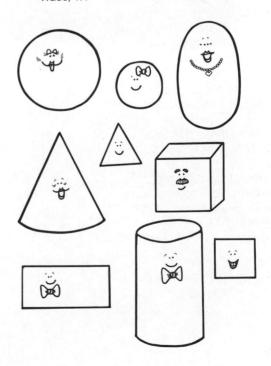

1-57029-521-2 *Piggyback Songs—School Days*

A Triangle

Sung to: Did You Ever See a Lassie?

        F   G7   F
Did you ever see a triangle, a triangle, a triangle?

Did you ever see a triangle?

  C7   F
It looks like a sail.

  C7   F   C7   F
It looks like a sail. It looks like a sail.

Did you ever see a triangle?

  C7   F
It looks like a sail.

Substitute a different word, such as tent, *for sail.*

> Priscilla M. Starrett
> Warren, PA

The Triangle Song

Sung to: Pop! Goes the Weasel

  D   A7   D
I am a small triangle.

         A7   D
I have three sides you see.

     A7   D
I also have three corners.

A7   D
They're just right for me.

> Rita Galloway
> Harlingen, TX

A Circle

Sung to: Did You Ever See a Lassie?

        F   C7   F
Did you ever see a circle, a circle, a circle?

Did you ever see a circle?

  C7   F
It looks like a ball.

  C7   F   C7   F
It looks like a ball. It looks like a ball.

Did you ever see a circle?

  C7   F
It looks like a ball.

Substitute a different word, such as plate, *for* ball.

> Priscilla M. Starrett
> Warren, PA

Circle Song

Sung to: Jingle Bells

F
Round circles, round circles, round circles to
    make.

C7   F   G7   C
Oh, what fun it is to draw round circles to shake.

     F
Oh, round circles, round circles, round circles to
    make.

C7   F   C7   F
Oh, what fun it is to draw round circles to shake.

After the children have made their circles, sing this song, hold them up, and shake them when the song says.

> Mary Kelleher
> Lynn, MA

Shapes—Triangle and Circle

A Square

Sung to: Did You Ever See a Lassie?

F
Did you ever see a square,

C7   F
A square, a square?

Did you ever see a square?

C7   F
It looks like a box.

C7   F
It looks like a box.

C7   F
It looks like a box.

Did you ever see a square?

C7   F
It looks like a box.

You may substitute cube *for* box.

Priscilla M. Starrett
Warren, PA

A Rectangle

Sung to: Did You Ever See a Lassie?

F
Did you ever see a rectangle,

C7   F
A rectangle, a rectangle?

Did you ever see a rectangle?

C7   F
It looks like a book.

C7   F
It looks like a book.

C7   F
It looks like a book.

Did you ever see a rectangle?

C7   F
It looks like a book.

Substitute a different word, such as door, *for* book.

Priscilla M. Starrett
Warren, PA

The Square Song

Sung to: You Are My Sunshine

C
I am a square, a lovely square.

F   C
I have four sides; they're all the same.

F   C
I have four corners, four lovely corners.

G7   C
I am a square. That is my name.

Rita Galloway
Harlingen, TX

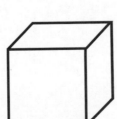

○ ○ ○ 𝟏 𝟐 𝟑 ◇ ▢ ◇ A B C ☆ ★ ☆ a b c

Draw a Circle

Sung to: Frere Jacques

C
✓ Draw a circle, draw a circle

Round as can be, round as can be.

Draw a circle, draw a circle

Just for me, just for me.
(Draw circle in air with finger.)

C
✓ Draw a rectangle, draw a rectangle

Shaped like a door, shaped like a door.

Draw a rectangle, draw a rectangle

With corners four, with corners four.
(Draw a rectangle in air with finger.)

C
Draw a triangle, draw a triangle

With corners three, with corners three.

Draw a triangle, draw a triangle

Just for me, just for me.
(Draw triangle in air with finger.)

Adapted Traditional

I Can Make a Shape

Sung to: Skip to My Lou

F
I can make a square, how about you?

C7
I can make a square, how about you?

F
I can make a square, how about you?

C7
Make a little square just like I do.
(Form square with fingers.)

Additional Verses: I can make a circle; a
triangle, a rectangle.

Jean Warren

Shapes in the Air

Sung to: The Mulberry Bush

C
This is a circle as you can see,
(Draw a circle in the air with your finger.)

G
You can see, you can see.

C
This is a circle as you can see.

   G   C
Now draw it in the air with me.

Repeat for other shapes.

Neoma Kreuter
Ontario, CA

Shapes—Draw

Shapes

Sung to: The Bear Went Over the Mountain

    C   F C
Un círculo hoy pintar-e-mos

    G7   C
Con un dedito en el aire.

                   F
Un círculo hoy pintar-emos,

C   G7   C
Dando la vuelta a-sí.
(Do actions as song indicates.)

Additional Verses: Un triángulo hoy
pintaremos; Un rectángulo hoy pintaremos;
Un cuadrado hoy pintaremos.

New Eton School Staff

Spanish Pronunciation

Oon SEER-koo-loh oy peen-tah-RAY-mohs
Kohn oon day-DEE-toh en ehl I-ray.
Oon SEER-koo-loh oy peen-tah-RAY-mohs,
DAHN-doh lah VWEHL-tah ah-SEE.

Additional Verses: Oon tree-AHN-goo-loh oy
peen-ta-RAY-mohs; Oon rek-TAHN-goo-loh oy
peen-ta-RAY-mohs; Oon kwah-DRAH-doh oy
peen-ta-RAY-mohs.

English Translation

Today we will draw a circle
In the air with a little finger.
Today we will draw a circle,
Going around like this.

Additional Verses: Today we will draw a
triangle; Today we will draw a rectangle; Today
we will draw a square.

The Shapes Are on the Floor

Sung to: The Farmer in the Dell

     D
The shapes are on the floor.

The shapes are on the floor.

Pick one up and guess its name,

    A7   D
And then we'll pick some more.

*Place a variety of shapes on the floor. As you
sing the song, have each child pick up a
shape. At the end of the song, have each
child name his or her shape, then put it back
on the floor.*

Lindsay Hall
Wytheville, VA

What Shape Is This?

Sung to: The Muffin Man

F
Do you know what shape this is,

    G7   C
What shape this is, what shape this is?

F
Do you know what shape this is

    G7   C   F
I'm holding in my hand?

*Sing the song several times, holding up a
different shape each time. Have the children
name the shape at the end of the song.*

Judy Hall
Wytheville, VA

Shapes—Draw

1-57029-521-2 *Piggyback Songs—School Days*

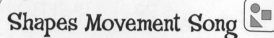

Shapes Movement Song

Sung to: Skip to My Lou

F
Jump, jump, jump to the circle.

C7
Jump, jump, jump to the circle.

F
Jump, jump, jump to the circle.

C7   F
Jump to the circle right now.
(Clap.)

F
Run, run, run to the square.

C7
Run, run, run to the square.

F
Run, run, run to the square.

C7   F
Run to the square right now.
(Clap.)

F
Roll, roll, roll to the triangle.

C7
Roll, roll, roll to the triangle.

F
Roll, roll, roll to the triangle.

C7   F
Roll to the triangle right now.
(Clap.)

*Before singing the song, tape a large paper
circle, square and triangle to the floor.*

Sue Yanchar
Kent, OH

Holding Shapes

Sung to: If You're Happy and You Know It

          G   D
If you're holding a square, stand up.

          G   G
If you're holding a square, stand up.

                    C
If there's a square in your hand,

                    G
Then it's time for you to stand.

          D   G
If you're holding a square, stand up.

*Repeat with additional verses about other
shapes.*

Judy Hall
Wytheville, VA

Sing a Song of Shapes

Sung to: Sing a Song of Sixpence

G
Sing a song of shapes.

D
Find them everywhere.

Sing a song of shapes.

G
Draw them in the air.

When you look for shapes

C
Hiding all around,

D
You will see a lot of shapes

          G
Are waiting to be found!

Gayle Bittinger

Counting Can Be So Much Fun

Sung to: Row, Row, Row Your Boat

C
One, two, three, four, five,

Six, seven, eight, nine, ten.

Counting can be so much fun.

Let's do it all again!

Substitute Now it's time to end *for* Let's do it all again *the last time you sing the song.*

> Neoma Kreuter
> Ontario, CA

Sing a Song of Numbers

Sung to: Sing a Song of Sixpence

C
Sing a song of numbers,

G7
Count them one by one.

Sing a song of numbers.

   C
We've only just begun.

One-two-three-four-five-six,

F
Seven-eight-nine-ten.

G7
When we finish counting them,

     C
We'll start them once a-gain.

> Judy Hall
> Wytheville, VA

I Can Count

Sung to: Frere Jacques

C
I can count. I can count.

One, two three; one two three.

I can count higher.

I can count higher.

Four five six; four five six.

C
I can count. I can count.

One, two, three, four five six.

I can count higher.

I can count higher.

Seven, eight, nine; seven, eight, nine.

C
I can count. I can count.

One, two, three, four, five, six.

I can count higher.

I can count higher.

Seven, eight, nine, ten, eleven, twelve.

> Saundra Winnett
> Lewisville, TX

1-57029-521-2 *Piggyback Songs—School Days*

○ ○ ○ 1 2 3 ◇ □ ◇ A B C ☆ ☆ ☆ a b c

✓ When the Numbers March [1 2 3] Right In

Sung to: When the Saints Go Marching In

           D
Oh, when the numbers march right in,

                             A7
Oh, when the numbers march right in,

    D   G
We will count them one by one,

        D   A7   D
When the numbers march right in.

           D
Oh, one-two-three and four-five-six,

                         A7
And seven-eight and nine and ten.

       D   G
When we finish all our numbers,

       D   A7   D
We will count them once a-gain.

Judy Hall
Wytheville, VA

✓ One, Two, Three [1 2 3]

Sung to: This Old Man

C
One, two, three, count with me.

F   G7
It's as easy as can be—

Four, five, six, seven, eight, nine, ten.

G7   C   G7 C
Now let's sing it once a-gain.

Judy Hall
Wytheville, VA

✓ Clap One, Two, Three [1 2 3]

Sung to: Row, Row, Row Your Boat

C
Clap, clap, clap your hands.

Clap them one, two, three.

The more you clap, the more we count,

So what will your count be?

One, two, three, four,

Five, six, seven.

The more you clap, the more we count:

Eight, nine, ten, eleven.

Adapted Traditional

✓ Numbers [1 2 3]

Sung to: Oh, My Darling Clementine

C
Count our numbers, count our numbers,

                       G7
Count our numbers every day.

                       C
It is fun to count our numbers

    G7   C
As a class, every day.

C
One-two-three-four, five-six-seven-eight,

                    G7
Nine and ten we'll count to-day.

                  C
It is fun to count to-gether,

    G7   C
One to ten and then a-gain.

Patricia Coyne
Mansfield, MA

Numbers—Counting

132

1-57029-521-2 *Piggyback Songs—School Days*

○ ○ ○ 1 2 3 ◇ ▢ ◇ A B C ☆ ☆ ☆ a b c

√ Give It a Shakey-Shakey

Sung to: Hokey Pokey

C
You put one finger up,

You put one finger down.

You put one finger up,

G
And you shake it all around.

You give it a shakey-shakey,

And you turn it all about—

C
That's how you learn to count.

C
You put two fingers up.

You put two fingers down.

You put two fingers up

G
And you shake them all around.

You give them a shakey-shakey,

And you turn them all about—

C
That's how you learn to count.

Continue with as many verses as desired, up to ten.

Lois Putnam
Pilot Mt., NC

One, Two, Three

Sung to: Frere Jacques

C
One, two, three; one, two three—

Sing with me. Sing with me.

One, two, three; one two three—

Sing with me. Sing with me.

C
Four, five, six; four, five, six—

Sing with me. Sing with me.

Four, five, six; four, five, six—

Sing with me. Sing with me.

Continue, counting up to twelve. You can also use letters of the alphabet instead of numbers when singing this song.

Jean Warren

One Rap, Two Rap

Sung to: Skip to My Lou

F
One rap, two rap, three rap, four.
(Rap fist.)

C7
Who's that rapping at my door?

F
Five rap, six rap, seven rap, eight.
(Rap fist.)

C7   F
Don't you think it's kind of late?

Jean Warren

1-57029-521-2 *Piggyback Songs—School Days*

Counting in Spanish

Sung to: *Three Blind Mice*

C   G   C   G   C
One, two, three; uno, dos, tres;

     G7   C   G7   C
Four, five, six; cuatro, cinco, seis.

         G   C
Counting in Spanish is fun to do.

        G   C
You sing with me, and I'll sing with you.

      G   C
Siete, ocho, nueve; seven, eight, nine.

G C   G C
Ten is diez. Ten is diez.

Vicki Shannon

Spanish Pronunciation

One two three; OO-noh, dohs, trays;
Four, five, six; KWAH-troh, SEEN-koh, sace.
Counting in Spanish is fun to do.
You sing with me, and I'll sing with you.
See-EH-tay, OH-choh, NWAY-vay; seven, eight,
   nine.
Ten is dee-EHS. Ten is dee-EHS.

English Translation

One, two, three; one, two, three;
Four, five, six; four five, six.
Counting in Spanish is fun to do.
You sing with me, and I'll sing with you.
Seven, eight, nine; seven, eight, nine.
Ten is ten. Ten is ten.

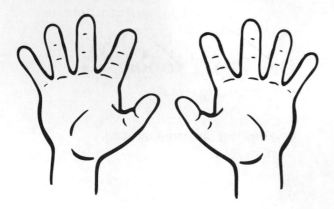

Rhyme Time

✓ One Potato

One potato, two potato,

Three potato, four.

Five potato, six potato,

Seven potato, more.

Traditional

Ten Little Toes

Sung to: This Old Man

C
I've got toes on my feet.

F   G7
Ten little toes; now, aren't they sweet?

              C
Let's count them now, all the way to ten.

G7   C   G7 C
Then we'll count all over a-gain.

> Margo S. Miller
> Westerville, OH

✓ Show Me One

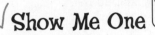

Sung to: Skip to My Lou

C
One, one, show me one.

G7
One, one, show me one.

C
One, one, show me one.

G7   C
Show me one right now.

Continue with as many verses as desired, up to ten.

> Lois Putnam
> Pilot Mt., NC

✓ Four Red Apples

Sung to: This Old Man

C
Four red apples on the tree,

F   G7
Two for you and two for me,

C   F   C
So-o shake that tree and watch them fall.

G7   C   G7 C
One, two, three, four. That is all.

> Jean Warren

Four Number Birds

Sung to: Twinkle, Twinkle, Little Star

C   F   C
One little bird flying in the blue.
(Hold up one finger.)

  G7   C   G7   C
A-long comes an-other, now there are two.
(Hold up two fingers.)

          G7   C   G7
Two little birds perched high in a tree.

  C   G7 C   G7
A-long comes an-other, now there are three.
(Hold up three fingers.)

C   F   C
Three little birds, see them swoop and soar.

  G7   C   G7   C
A-long comes an-other, and that makes four.
(Hold up four fingers.)

> Diane Thom
> Maple Valley, WA

1-57029-521-2 *Piggyback Songs—School Days*

Numbers

We Found a Letter 🔤

Sung to: The Farmer in the Dell

    D
We found a *B* today.

We found a *B* today.

B, B, we found a *B.*

   A7   D
We found a *B* to-day!

Substitute the name of any letter for B.

    Gayle Bittinger

Where Has Our 🔤 Letter Gone?

Sung to: Where, Oh, Where Has My Little Dog Gone?

C   G
Where, oh, where has our letter *A* gone?

  G7   C
Oh where, oh where can it be?

                   G7
It is on a card that we had all along.

                    C
Won't you find it and show it to me?

Hide index cards with letters written on them around the room. As you sing the song, have the children look for the letter you name.

    Judy Hall
    Wytheville, VA

✓ ABC Song 🔤

Sung to: Twinkle, Twinkle, Little Star

C   F   C
A is for alligator, airplane and ants.

G7   C   G7   C
A is for astronaut doing a dance.

      G7   C   G7
B is for ball and block and bee.

C   G7   C   G7
B is for baby, waving at me.

C   F   C
C is for crayons, car and cat.

G7   C   G7   C
C is for clown in a funny striped hat.

    Jean Warren

✓ Found a Letter 🔤

Sung to: Found a Peanut

          F
Found a letter, found a letter,

               C7
Found a letter *A* to-day.

                 F
Oh, today I found a letter,

      C7   F
Found a letter *A* to-day.

Substitute other letters as desired.

    Judy Hall
    Wytheville, VA

Alphabet Song

Sung to: The ABC Song
(Alternating A & B Sections)

```
C              F        C
A is for apple, B is for ball;

G7      C    G7      C
C is for candy, D is for doll.

        G7        C      G7
E is for elephant, F is for frog;

C       G7      C       G7
G is for goose, H is for hog.

C              F        C
I is for Indian, J is for jam;

G7     C  G7      C
K is for key, L is for lamb.

        G7        C      G7
M is for monkey, N is for nail;

C       G7 C      G7
O is for owl, P is for pail.

C              F        C
Q is for queen, R is for rose;

G7      C       G7      C
S is for scissors, T is for toes.

        G7      C       G7
U is for um-brella, V is for vase;

G7      C             G7   C
W is for wind blowing in my face.

C              F        C
X is for X-ray, Y is for you;

G7      C   G7     C
Z is for zebra in the zoo.
```

Marie Wheeler
Tacoma, WA

Picking Up an A

Sung to: The Paw Paw Patch

```
F
Picking up an A and putting it in the basket,

C7
Picking up an A and putting it in the basket,

F
Picking up an A and putting it in the basket,

C7                          F
Way down yonder in the letter patch.
```

Write alphabet letters on index cards and place the cards on the floor. Put a basket in the middle of the floor. As you sing the song, have the children pick up cards with the letter A written on them and put them in the basket. Continue with other letters as desired.

Judy Hall
Wytheville, VA

I Found a Letter

Sung to: Skip to My Lou

```
F
I found an A, how about you?

C
I found an A, how about you?

F
I found an A, how about you?

C                    F
I found an A, and you can, too.
```

Substitute the name of any letter for A.

Elizabeth McKinnon

Published by Totline Publications. Copyright protected.

1-57029-521-2 *Piggyback Songs—School Days*

Letters

○ ○ ○ 1 2 3 ◇ ◻ ◇ **A B C** ☆ ☆ ☆ **a b c**

Do You Know 🗨 Your Opposites?

Sung to: Did You Ever See a Lassie?

F
Do you know your opposites,

    C7   F
Your opposites, your opposites?

Do you know your opposites?

    C7   F
Then sing some with me.

      C7   F
There's up and down;

      C7   F
There's lost and found.

Do you know your opposites?

    C7   F
Then sing some with me.

F
Do you know your opposites,

    C7   F
Your opposites, your opposites?

Do you know your opposites?

    C7   F
Then sing some with me.

      C7   F
There's in and out;

      C7   F
There's whisper and shout.

Do you know your opposites?

    C7   F
Then sing some with me.

Additional Verses: There's hot and cold,
there's young and old; There's fast and slow,
there's stop and go; There's day and night,
there's left and right.

Janice Bodenstedt
Jackson, MI

Opposites 🗨

Sung to: Mary Had a Little Lamb

C
Up and down are opposites,

G   C
Opposites, opposites.

Up and down are opposites

G7   C
That we learned to-day.

*Use hand motions where possible, or actions,
and see how many opposites you can sing
about. Suggestions: hard and soft, big and
little, black and white, etc.*

Lynn Beaird
Lompoc, CA

○ ○ ○ 1 2 3 □ □ ◇ A B C ☆ ★ ☆ a b c

It Opens and Closes

Sung to: Did You Ever See a Lassie?

       F
Have you ever seen a door,

 C7   F
A door, a door?

Have you ever seen a door

   C7   F
That works like this?

   C7   F
It opens and closes,

   C7   F
It opens and closes.

Have you ever seen a door

    C7   F
That works like this?

Repeat, each time substituting the name of a different item that opens and closes for door.

      Elizabeth McKinnon

Quiet and Noisy

Sung to: Row, Row, Row Your Boat

C
Let's sing a quiet song,

Let's whisper it today.

Let's make our voices, oh, so soft

As we sing today.

C
Let's sing a noisy song.

Let's shout it out this way.

Let's make our voices, oh, so loud

As we sing today!

      Elizabeth McKinnon

Right Hand, Left Hand

Sung to: Mary Had a Little Lamb

C
My right hand touches my right foot,
(Touch right hand to body parts named.)

G7   C
My right knee, my right eye.

My right hand touches my right ear,

G7   C
All on my right side.

C
My left hand touches my left foot,
(Touch left hand to body parts named.)

G7   C
My left knee, my left eye.

My left hand touches my left ear,

G7   C
All on my left side.

      Laura Egge
      Lake Oswego, OR

○ ○ ○ ○ 𝟏 𝟐 𝟑 ◇ ▢ ◆ A B C ☆ ★ ☆ a b c

Little and Big

Sung to: Twinkle, Twinkle, Little Star

C   F   C
Pequeño is little; grande is big.

   G7   C G7   C
No matter if it's a tree or a twig.

     G7   C   G7
Pequeño is little; grande is big.

C   G7   C   G7
Great big hog or baby pig.

C   F   C
Pequeño is little; grande is big,

   G7   C G7   C
No matter if it's a tree or a twig.

Diane Thom

Spanish Pronunciation

Peh-KEHN-yoh is little; GRAHN-day is big.
No matter if it's a tree or a twig.
Peh-KEHN-yoh is little; GRAHN-day is big.
Great big hog or baby pig.
Peh-KEHN-yoh is little; GRAHN-day is big,
No matter if it's a tree or a twig.

English Translation

Little is little; big is big,
No matter if it's a tree or a twig.
Little is little; big is big.
Great big hog or baby pig.
Little is little; big is big,
No matter if it's a tree or a twig.

Up and Down

Sung to: Here We Go Looby Loo

D
See us reach up, up, up;

                               A7
See us reach down, down, down.

D
See us reach up, up, up.

A7   D
Now see us twirl all a-round.

Elizabeth McKinnon

Empty and Full

Sung to: Row, Row, Row Your Boat

C
Fill, fill, fill the bag.

Fill it now with me.

First it's empty, then it's full,

Full as full can be.

Elizabeth McKinnon

The Big, Round Clock

Sung to: The Wheels on the Bus

F
The big, round clock goes tick-tick-tock,

C   F
Tick-tick-tock, tick-tick-tock.

The big, round clock goes tick-tick-tock,

   C   F
To tell us the time.

     F
The hands on the clock go 'round and 'round,

C   F
'Round and 'round, 'round and 'round.

The hands on the clock go 'round and 'round

   C   F
To tell us the time.

Barbara Paxson
Warren, OH

The Hands Are On the Clock

Sung to: Hickory Dickory Dock

C   G7   C
Hickory, dickory dock—

        G7   C
The hands are on the clock.

              F
One is long, the other's short—

C   G7   C
Hickory, dickory dock.

Judy Hall
Wytheville, VA

The Little Clock

Sung to: I'm a Little Teapot

C   F   C
I'm a little clock up on the wall.

G7   C
Here is my big hand,

G7   C
Here is my small.

If you listen carefully,

F   C
You will hear,

        F   G7   C
Tick-tock, tick-tock, in your ear.

Judy Hall
Wytheville, VA

A Clock's Face

Sung to: Twinkle, Twinkle, Little Star

C   F   C
My clock has a great big face,

G7   C   G7   C
With hands moving from the nose place.

        G7   C   G7
The hour hand moves slowly 'round.

      C   G7   C   G7
From 1 to 12 with a tick-tock sound.

       C   F   C
The hour hand won't say o'clock

      G7   C   G7 C
'Til the minute hand makes 60 tocks.

Ellen Bedford
Bridgeport, CT

1-57029-521-2 *Piggyback Songs—School Days*

Time—Clocks

Do You Know What Time It Is?

Sung to: The Muffin Man

F
Do you know what time it is,

     G7   C
What time it is, what time it is?

F
Do you know what time it is?

G7 C   F
Look at the clock.

     F
The big hand is on the number 12,

     G7   C
The number 12, the number 12.

     F
The big hand is on the number 12

G7 C   F
On our big clock.

     F
The small hand is on the number 2,

     G7   C
The number 2, the number 2.

     F
The small hand is on the number 2

G7 C   F
On our big clock.

F
That means it is two o'clock,

G7   C
Two o'clock, two o'clock.

F
That means it is two o'clock.

G7   C   F
Time to go out-side.

Substitute the names of the appropriate numbers, time and activity for the ones in the song.

Cindy Dingwall
Palatine, IL

Clock Song

Sung to: Hickory, Dickory Dock

C   G7   C
Hickory, dickory, dock.

      G7   C
The time is one o'clock.

See the little hand

F
Point to one.

C   G7   C
Hickory, dickory, dock.

As you continue with similar verses, naming hours up to 12 o'clock, hold up a play clock and move the hands to the appropriate times.

Elizabeth McKinnon

Time—Telling Time

142

School Time

Sung to: Frere Jacques

C
What time's school time?

What time's school time

On the clock, on the clock?

Show us when it's school time.

Show us when it's school time

On the clock, on the clock.

Set out a play clock and have the children take turns showing you the time.

Additional Verses: What time's snack time?
What time's lunchtime? What time's rest time?
What time's playtime?, etc.

Betty Silkunas
Lansdale, PA

My Little Watch

Sung to: Twinkle, Twinkle, Little Star

C   F   C
See my little watch right here?
(Form circle with thumb and finger.)

G7   C   G7   C
Hold it closely to your ear.
(Hold circle up to ear.)

C   G7   C   G7
Hear it ticking, ticking fast.

   C   G7   C   G7
It tells us when our playtime's past.

C   F   C
See my little watch right here.
(Motions as before.)

G7   C   G7   C
Hold it closely to your ear.

Repeat, each time substituting a different event, such as story time *or* snack time *for* playtime.

Adapted Traditional

What Time Is It?

Sung to: The Muffin Man

F
Do you know what time it is,

   G7   C
What time it is, what time it is?

F
Do you know what time it is?

G7   C   F
Let's look and see.

        F
It's 12 o'clock and all is well.

   G7   C
It's 12 o'clock and all is well.

        F
It's 12 o'clock and all is well.

G7   C   F
All is well to-day.

Substitute the name of the actual time for the words 12 o'clock.

Judy Hall
Wytheville, VA

1-57029-521-2 *Piggyback Songs—School Days*

Time—Time for...

What Time Is It?

Sung to: Billy Boy

C
¿Qué hora es, Nicolette, Nicolette?

G7
¿Qué hora es, Nico-lette?

¿Es hora de acostarse?

C
¿Es hora de acostarse?

C   G7   C
¿Qué hora es, Nico-lette?

Substitute the names of your children and the different activities of the day for Nicolette *and* acostarse.

sing	cantar	cahn-TAHR
eat	comer	koh-MEHR
play	jugar	hoo-GAHR
paint	pintar	peen-TAHR
dance	bailar	bi-LAHR

Sonya Kranwinkel

Spanish Pronunciation

Kay OHR-ah ehs, Nicolette, Nicolette?
Kay OHR-ah ehs, Nicolette?
Ehs OHR-ah day ah-koh-STAHR-say?
Ehs OHR-ah day ah-koh-STAHR-say?
Kay OR-ah ehs, Nicolette?

English Translation

What time is it, Nicolette, Nicolette?
What time is it, Nicolette?
Is it time to lie down?
Is it time to lie down?
What time is it, Nicolette?

The Clock Goes 'Round Each Day

Sung to: Row, Row, Row Your Boat

C
Tick, tock, tick-tock-tick.

The clock goes 'round each day.

It tell us when it's time to work

And when it's time to play.

Adapted Traditional

Time

Sung to: Ten Little Indians

C
One o'clock, two o'clock, three o'clock hour,

G
Four o'clock, five o'clock, six o'clock hour,

C
Seven o'clock, eight o'clock, nine o'clock hour,

G7   C
Ten, eleven, and twelve.

Judy Hall
Wytheville, VA

Time

○ ○ ○ 1 2 3 ◇ ▢ ◇ A B C ☆ ★ ☆ a b c

Calendar Song

Sung to: The Mulberry Bush

C
The calendar shows the name of the month,

G   C
The name of the month, the name of the month.

The calendar shows the name of the month,

G   C
For every month of the year.

C
The calendar shows the days of the week,

G
The days of the week, the days of the week.

C
The calendar shows the days of the week,

G   C
For every month of the year.

C
The calendar shows the dates of the month,

G
The dates of the month, the dates of the month.

C
The calendar shows the dates of the month,

G   C
For every month of the year.

C
To-day is the first day of the month,

G
Day of the month, day of the month.

C
To-day is the first day of the month,

G   C
Of the month of Sep-tember.

*Substitute the appropriate date and month for
the words* first *and* September.

Darlene Bursch
San Jose, CA

The Calendar

Sung to: Twinkle, Twinkle, Little Star

C   F   C
When we do the calen-dar,

G7   C   G7   C
We learn the month, the date and year.

G7   C   G7
Every weekday has a name.

C   G7   C   G7
And lots of numbers look the same.

C   G   C
So let's begin to show you how.

G7   C   G7   C
We do the calen-dar right now.

Susan Burbridge
Beavercreek, OH

 1-57029-521-2 *Piggyback Songs—School Days*

Calendar

○ ○ ○ 1 2 3 ◇ □ ◇ A B C ☆ ☆ ☆ a b c

✓ Oh, If You Know the Month ☀

Sung to: If You're Happy and You Know It

    F   C
Oh, if you know the month, shout it out. *

    C   F
Oh, if you know the month, shout it out. *

      Bb
Oh, if you know the month,

    F
Oh, if you know the month,

    C   F
Oh, if you know the month, shout it out. *

    F   C
Oh, if you know the day, whisper it now. *

    C   F
Oh, if you know the day, whisper it now. *

      Bb
Oh, if you know the day,

    F
Oh, if you know the day,

    C   F
Oh, if you know the day, whisper it now. *

    F   C
Oh, if you know the date, shout it out. *

    C   F
Oh, if you know the date, shout it out. *

      Bb
Oh, if you know the date,

    F
Oh, if you know the date,

    C   F
Oh, if you know the date, shout it out. *

Have the students say the names of the present month, day and date.

Sharon K. Engel
Oshkosh, WI

Yesterday, Today and Tomorrow ☀

Sung to: Frere Jacques

C
Monday, Monday, Monday, Monday,

All day long, all day long.

Yesterday was Sunday;

Tomorrow will be Tuesday.

Oh, what fun; oh, what fun.

Substitute the names of the appropriate days for the words Monday, Sunday *and* Tuesday.

Linda Ferguson
Olympia, WA

AUGUST						
S	M	T	W	TH	F	S
1	2	3	4	5	6	7
8	9	10	11	12	13	14
15	16	17	18	19	20	21
22	23	24	25	26	27	28
29	30	31				

○ ○ ○ 1 2 3 ◇ □ ◇ A B C ☆ ☆ ☆ a b c

✓ Months of the Year

Sung to: Skip to My Lou

F
Come and sing along with me.

C7
Come and sing along with me.

F
Come and sing along with me

    C7   F
The twelve months of the year.

F
January, February, March, and April,

C7
May, June, July, and August,

F
September, October, November, December

C7   F
Are the twelve months of the year.

      Karen M. Smith
      Bluemont, VA

Months

Sung to: Ten Little Indians

C
January, February, March and April,

G7
May and June and July and August,

C
September, October, November, December,

G7   C
Now we've said them all.

      Florence Dieckmann
      Roanoke, VA

The Months of the Year

Sung to: Three Blind Mice

C   G7   C
January, February, March,

      G7   C
April, May, June.

      G7   C
July, August, Sep-tember,

        G7   C
October, No-vember, De-cember.

        G7   C
These are the twelve months of the year.

        G7   C
Now sing them to-gether so we can all hear.

        G7   C
How many months are there in a year?

        G7   C
Twelve months in a year.

      Laura Copeland
      Homewood, IL

Calendar—Months

147

1-57029-521-2 Piggyback Songs—School Days

The Months of the Year

Sung to: Ten Little Indians

C
Enero, febrero, marzo, y abril,

G7
Mayo, junio, julio, y agosto,

C
Septiembre, octubre, noviembre, y
    diciembre—

G7   C
These are the months of the year.

C
January, February, March, and April,

G7
May, June, July, and August,

C
September, October, November, and
    December—

G7   C
These are the months of the year.

Diane Thom

Spanish Pronunciation

Eh-NEHR-oh, feh-BREH-roh, MAHR-zoh, ee
    ah-BREEL,
MAH-yoh, HOO-nee-oh, HOO-lee-oh, ee
    ah-GOHS-toh,
Sehp-tee-EHM-bray, ohk-TOO-bray, noh-vee-
    EHM-bray, ee dee-see-EHM-bray—
These are the months of the year.

January, February, March, and April,
May, June, July, and August,
September, October, November, and
    December—
These are the months of the year.

English Translation

January, February, March, and April,
May, June, July, and August,
September, October, November, and
    December—
These are the months of the year.

January, February, March, and April,
May, June, July, and August,
September, October, November, and
    December—
These are the months of the year.

Count the Days

Sung to: Twinkle, Twinkle, Little Star

C   F   C
Come along and count with me.

G7   C   G7   C
There are seven days, you see.

        G7   C   G7
Sunday, Monday, Tuesday, too,

C   G7   C   G7
Wednesday, Thursday, just for you.

C   F   C
Friday, Saturday, that's the end.

G7   C   G7   C
Now let's sing our song a-gain!

Judy Hall
Wytheville, VA

1-57029-521-2 *Piggyback Songs—School Days*

Calendar—Months and Days

Seven Days in a Week

Sung to: For He's a Jolly Good Fellow

        F   Bb F
Oh, there's seven days in a we-ek,

C   F
Seven days in a week,

        Bb
Seven days in a week,

    F   C7   F
And I can say them all.

F   Bb F
Sunday, Monday, and Tues-day,

C   F
Wednesday, Thursday, and Friday,

F   Bb
Saturday is the last day,

    F   C7   F
And I can say them all.

Darla Carson
Ellinwood, KS

There Are Seven

Sung to: Pop! Goes the Weasel

D   A   D
Sunday, Monday, Tuesday, Wednesday,

            A   D
Thursday, Friday, Saturday.

         A   D
Do you know what day it is?

A   D
Yes, it is Thursday.

D   A   D
Sunday, Monday, Tuesday, Wednesday,

            A   D
Thursday, Friday, Saturday.

         A   D
Do you know how many there are?

A   D
Yes, there are seven.

Substitute the name of the appropriate day for the word Thursday.

Ann-Marie Donovan
Framingham, MA

Every Week

Sung to: London Bridge

C
Every week has seven days,

G   C
Seven days, seven days.

Every week has seven days.

G   C
Can you name them?

C
Sunday, Monday, Tuesday, Wednesday,

G7   C
Thursday, Friday, Saturday.

Sunday, Monday, Tuesday, Wednesday,

G   C
Thursday, Friday, Saturday.

Rita Galloway
Harlingen, TX

149

1-57029-521-2 *Piggyback Songs—School Days*

The Days of the Week

Sung to: Did You Ever See a Lassie?

F   C7   F
Can-temos de los días de la se-mana,

                C7   F
Cantemos de los días de la se-mana.

    C7   F
El do-mingo, el lunes,

    C7   F
El martes, el miércoles,

             C7   F
El jueves, el viernes, y el sába-do.

Diane Thom

Spanish Pronunciation

Kahn-TEH-mohs day lohs DEE-ahs day lah
   say-MAH-nah,
Kahn-TEH-mohs day lohs DEE-ahs day lah
   say-MAH-nah.
Ehl doh-MEEN-goh, ehl LOON-nehs, ehl
   MAHR-tehs, ehl mee-EHR-koh-lehs,
Ehl HWAY-bays, ehl vee-EHR-nehs, ee
   ehl SAH-bah-doh.

English Translation

Let's sing about the days of the week,
Let's sing about the days of the week.
Sunday, Monday, Tuesday, Wednesday,
Thursday, Friday, and Saturday.

Days of the Week

Sung to: Yankee Doodle

C   G7
Sunday, Monday, Tuesday, Wednesday,

C   G7
Thursday, Friday, Satur-day.

     C   F
Don't ask me not to sing again,

   G7   C
Be-cause I'll do it anyway!

F
Sunday, Monday, Tuesday, Wednesday,

C
Thursday, Friday, Saturday.

F
Sunday, Monday, Tuesday, Wednesday,

C   G7   C
Thursday, Friday, Saturday.

Laura Egge
Lake Oswego, OR

Days

Sung to: Frere Jacques

C
Sunday, Monday, Tuesday, Wednesday,

And Thursday, and Friday.

Don't forget the last day;

Don't forget the last day:

Saturday. Let's all play!

Deborah A Roessel
Flemington, NJ

Calendar—Days

Published by Totline Publications. Copyright protected.

1-57029-521-2 *Piggyback Songs—School Days*

○ ○ ○ 1 2 3 ◇ ◇ ◇ A B C ☆ ☆ ☆ a

Day Song

Sung to: Skip to My Lou

C
Hey, hey, what do you say?

G7
Hey, hey, what do you say?

C
Hey, hey, what do you say,

G7   C
For today's a ___-day.

C
Hey, hey, let's join hands.

G7
Hey, hey, let's join hands.

C
Hey, hey, let's join hands

G7   C
While we sit and make our plans.

Fill in the name of the day of the week.

Jean Warren

Don't Forget the Day

Sung to: You Are My Sunshine

     C
Today is Friday; it's really Friday,

    F   C
From early morning, 'til late at night.

    F   C
While we are working, while we are playing,

    G7   C
Don't forget it's Friday to-day.

*Substitute the name of the appropriate day for
the word Friday.*

Ellen Javernick
Loveland, CO

Today Is

Sung to: Mary Had a Little Lamb

F   C   F
To-day is ___-day, ___-day, ___-day;

        C   F
To-day is ___- day. Let's all sing a song.

F   C   F
It will be a fun day, fun day, fun day.

        C   F
It will be a fun day, all day long.

F   C   F
Sing a song of ___-day, ___-day, ___-day;

        C   F
Sing a song of ___-day, all day long.

*For both Day Song and Today Is, fill in blanks
with whatever type of day it is. For example:*

Monday	good day	red day
Tuesday	new day	blue day
Wednesday	sunny day	round day
Thursday	birthday	square day
Friday	holiday	etc.

Jean Warren

What Day Is It?

Sung to: Mary Had a Little Lamb

C
Do you know what day it is,

G7   C
Day it is, day it is?

Do you know what day it is?

G7   C
Today is Tues-day.

*Substitute the appropriate day for the word
Tuesday.*

Betty Ruth Baker
Waco, TX

1-57029-521-2 *Piggyback Songs—School Days*

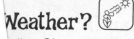

What's the Weather?

Sung to: Oh, My Darling Clementine

What's the weather? What's the weather?

                  G7
What's the weather, every-one?

         C
Is it windy? Is it cloudy?

  G7   C
Is there rain, or is there sun?

      Betty Silkunas
      Lansdale, PA

✓ Rain on My Umbrella

Sung to: Frere Jacques

C
Drip, drip, drop, drop; drip, drip, drop, drop;

Drip, drip, drop; drip, drip, drop.

Rain on my umbrella

Rain on my umbrella

Never stop.

Drip, drip, drop.

      Betty Silkunas
      Lansdale, PA

Look Out the Window

Sung to: Frere Jacques

C
What's the weather? What's the weather,

On this Monday, on this Monday?

Let's look out the window.

Let's look out the window.

It is sunny. It is sunny.

Substitute the name of the appropriate day of the week and the type of weather for the ones in the song.

      Cindy Dingwall
      Palatine, IL

✓ The Wind Is Blowing

Sung to: Mary Had a Little Lamb

   C
The wind is blowing all around,

G7   C
All around, all around.

The wind is blowing all around,

G7   C
All around the town.

      Judith McNitt
      Adrian, MI

Weather

○ ○ ○ 1 2 3 ◇ □ ◇ A B C ☆ ☆ ☆ a b c

Four Seasons

Sung to: Twinkle, Twinkle, Little Star

C   F   C
Flowers, swimming, pumpkins, snow,

G7   C   G7   C
Make the seasons we all know.

     G7   C   G7
Every year it is the same;

C   G7   C   G7
And we give them each a name.

C   F   C
Summer, autumn, winter, spring:

G7   C   G7   C
Count the seasons as we sing.

Mrs. Bill Dean
Richland, WA

Sing a Song of Springtime

Sung to: Sing a Song of Sixpence

C   G7
Sing a song of springtime. Birds fill the air.

Plants are sprouting up again,

     C
And the weather's fair.

                 G7
The sun is bright and warm with blossoms on
   the way.

                 C
Isn't it time for a wonderful spring day?

Elizabeth Vollrath
Stevens Pt., WI

In the Fall

Sung to: She'll Be Coming 'Round the Mountain

        F
Oh, the leaves turn brown and yellow in the fall.

                              C7
Oh, the leaves turn brown and yellow in the fall.

        F
Oh, the leaves turn brown and yellow,

        B♭
Yes, the leaves turn brown and yellow,

        F   C7   F
Oh, the leaves turn brown and yellow in the fall.

Betty Silkunas
Lansdale, PA

Summer Fun

Sung to: Frere Jacques

C
It is summer. It is summer:

Lots of fun, lots of fun;

Swimming, picnics, playing;

Swimming, picnics, playing.

I'll have fun. I'll have fun.

Rose Lucio
Garden Grove, CA

Published by Totline Publications. Copyright protected.

1-57029-521-2 *Piggyback Songs—School Days*

Seasons

Did You Ever See It?

Sung to: Did You Ever See a Lassie?

      F
Did you ever see a shape,
(Adult sings while pointing to a shape.)

   C7   F
A shape, a shape?

Did you ever see a shape

    C7   F
Like this one be-fore?

    C7   F
The shape is a _____.
(Everyone sings.)

    C7   F
The shape is a _____.

Oh, yes, we've seen a shape

    C7   F
Like that one be-fore.

Substitute a different word, such as color, number, letter, *or* animal, *for* shape.

     Laura Egge
     Lake Oswego, OR

Oh, Do You Know?

Sung to: The Muffin Man

      G
Oh, do you know what color this is,
(Adult sings while pointing to a color.)

     C   D7
What color this is, what color this is?

      G
Oh, do you know what color this is?

     D7   G
Please tell me, if you know.
(Children respond.)

Substitute a different word, such as shape, number, letter, *or* animal, *for* color.

     Laura Egge
     Lake Oswego, OR

What Is It?

Sung to: Jimmy Crack Corn

F   C7
What is the number I have here?
(Adult sings while pointing to a number.)

                F
_____ is the number you have there.
(Children respond.)

              B♭
You knew the answer to that one.
(Adult sings.)

   C7   F
So now I'll ask one more.

Substitute a different word, such as color, shape, letter, *or* animal, *for* number. *For the final verse of the song, end with* So now I'll ask no more.

     Laura Egge
     Lake Oswego, OR

Multiple Concepts

    1-57029-521-2 *Piggyback Songs—School Days*

The Guessing Game

Sung to: Mary Had a Little Lamb

C
My friend has a green shirt on,

G7   C
Green shirt on, green shirt on.

My friend has a green shirt on.

G7   C
Can you name my friend?

Substitute the name of the color and the item of clothing one of the children is wearing for the words green shirt. *Have the children try to guess which child it is.*

Ann-Marie Donovan
Framingham, MA

✓ Count to Three

Sung to: Mary Had a Little Lamb

C
Lightly tap your foot two times,
(Tap twice with the words "two times")

G   C
Foot two times, foot two times.

C
Lightly tap your foot two times.

G   C
Now let's count to three.

C
One, two, three, let's all sit down,

G   C
All sit down, all sit down.

C
One, two, three, let's all sit down,

G   C
Gently on the ground.

Barb Robinson
Huntington Beach, CA

One Blue Square

Sung to: Three Blind Mice

C   G7   C
One blue square,

C   G7   C
One blue square—

   G7   C
See how it's shaped.

   G7   C
See how it's shaped.

Four big corners it does have.

Four big corners it does have.

Four big corners it does have.

   G7   C
One blue square.

Mary Kelleher
Lynn, MA

Do You Know?

Sung to: The Mulberry Bush

D
Children, children, do you know,
(Adult sings while holding up a letter.)

A7
Do you know, do you know;

D
Children, children, do you know

The letter I'm holding up?
(Children name letter.)

Substitute a different word, such as color, shape, number, *or* animal, *for* letter.

Laura Egge
Lake Oswego, OR

Multiple Concepts

1-57029-521-2 *Piggyback Songs—School Days*

Dear Parents,

Sing a song with your child, and several great things happen: You have a merry time together, your child learns, and you pass along a love for music. In fact, music is a fun and important part of life, and now is a critical time in your child's musical development. These early childhood years are the perfect time to make music with your child.

Did you know that music instruction and enrichment are not just for school? Home is also a fantastic place to work with your child and foster his or her musical development. You can do this by creating an environment filled with opportunities for musical experience, exploration, and expression.

To provide musical experience, begin by playing or singing a wide variety of music for your child. Expose him or her to different sounds, instruments (real and homemade), styles, and voices. Don't limit yourself to only children's songs, but when you do play and sing music specifically designed for children, include a range of soloists, groups, languages, and cultures. There are also many great children's books that are based on or include songs. Take the time to notice and listen to music all around you!

For exploration, you may set up a little listening corner, with different music your child can choose and play independently. Gather instruments and household items such as pots, cans, and tubs for your child to experiment with different sounds and rhythms. Take every chance you get to encourage musical curiosity and creativity.

Musical expression comes naturally to many children, as they use the musical elements they have experienced and explored to communicate. Model and participate in making up music to play. Sing with your child about little things throughout your day. Use your own tune or choose an old familiar tune and put your own words to it.

Music development is a fun and rewarding experience that will benefit you and your child, so get involved and enjoy making music!

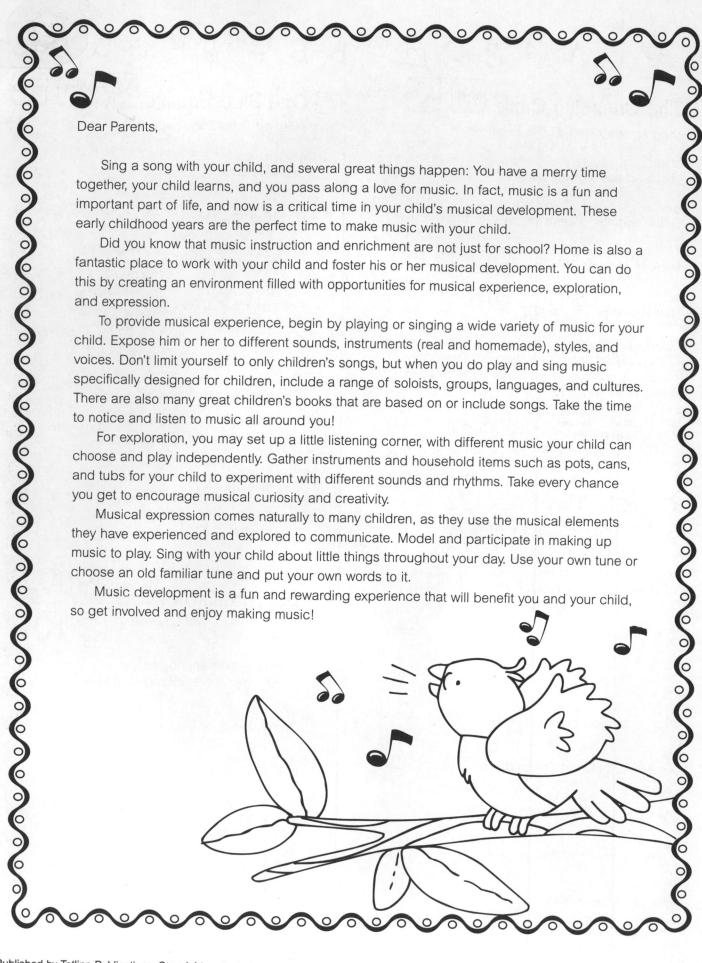

Teacher: Use this page to share songs with parents. Copy the song or songs you have used and paste them on this page, making copies to send home. You may even choose to make "Music We Know" compilation folders. To make these, get a pocket folder with brads for each student. Write their name and a title like "Music We Know" on the cover. As you learn new songs, copy them onto this page, hole-punch them, and put them in the folders. Then send home the folders on a weekly, monthly, or quarterly basis to encourage music at home.

✂ -

Today at school I learned this song, now we can sing it all day long.

Literacy Connection Ideas

Below are some ideas for ways you can use Piggyback songs to address early childhood literacy standards.

Phonological Awareness
Missing Words
To work on matching sound and rhymes, pause before saying the rhyming word at the end of a line. Allow children singing along to predict and anticipate words that may complete the line. Prompt them by singing the previous line with emphasis on the word that is to be rhymed with. For fun, substitute other rhyming words in the song to make it a "silly rhyme song."

See-the-Sound
To work on associating sounds with written words, write out some of the songs on chart paper or sentence strips. Pick out words that start with a sound you want to emphasize and write them on sticky notes or note cards. (Use a different color for the beginning sound to make your chosen letters stand out more.) Cover each word in the song with its sticky note or card. Before singing, point out the special sounds. During singing, emphasize the special sounds. And after singing, move the words onto their own list or chart titled "Words that start with the __ sound."

Print Awareness and Concepts
Follow-Along Songs
Choose slow songs that are easy to follow along with and copy them onto chart paper. As you sing, model basic concepts of print, such as left to right and top to bottom directionality. Also build the association between spoken and written words by deliberately pointing to each word as it is sung. On very slow songs, after modeling this following along a few times, allow student volunteers to come up and follow along with each word as you sing it.

Word Crunch / Mystery Word
To work on recognizing a word as a unit of print, begin by choosing a song to write out on sentence strips. Then cut apart each word and place them in a pocket chart with no spaces between the words. Show this "word crunch" song to the students before singing and ask, "What is wrong with this song?" Lead them to discuss and recognize that words need to be separated by spaces. Another way of emphasizing that words have meaning is to flip over a few words in your song so the blank side of the sentence strip is showing. As you sing, stop at each mystery word and have students use rhyme or context clues to figure out what the word may be before turning it over to solve the mystery.

Early Writing
Make-a-Verse
To work on writing as communication and experimenting with various writing tools, choose a song with opportunities for creating additional verses. Pass out sentence strips and allow children to "write" their own verses to go with the song, representing their ideas with pictures, letters, scribbles, etc. Write the song on chart paper or sentence strips, and attach students' verses at the bottom. (You may also want to write a "teacher version" of their song in correct spelling and grammar to post next to each student verse.)

Alphabet Knowledge
L-E-T-T-E-R-S
To work on associating names of letters with their shapes and sounds, write out songs that follow the "B-I-N-G-O" pattern. Emphasize each letter as it is sung, and call up students before or after singing to point to a given letter. You may also write letter cards for designated students to hold up when their letter is sung.

Book Knowledge and Appreciation
Mini-Books
To provide opportunities for retelling and dictating stories from books, make narrative songs into mini-books. Copy the template on page 159 and write in the words to a song your class has learned. Reproduce as mini-books for students and allow them to illustrate the story as you read/sing it. When finished, send these books home for children to share with their families.

Mini-Book Template

1

4

2

3

1-57029-521-2 *Piggyback Songs—School Days*

Sign Language Alphabet and Numbers

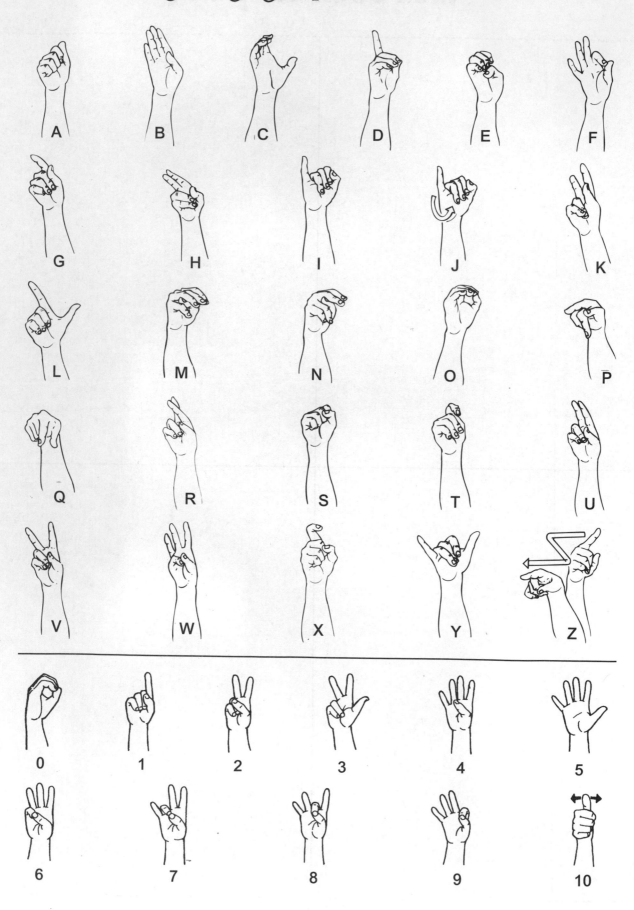

1-57029-521-2 *Piggyback Songs—School Days*